SEDONA CALLING

A Guide to Red Rock Country

By Lawrence W. Cheek

Photography by
Arizona Highways Contributors

ARIZONA
HIGHWAYS

CONTENTS

These images, also seen in the five chapters of this book, represent a photographic summary. From left: Paradise Found — an overview of red rock country. Inside Sedona — artistic moods flourish. Outside Sedona — terrain suited for active recreation. Day Trips — ancient ruins are on the itinerary. Farther Out — overnighters to the Grand Canyon and elsewhere.

Sedona Calling brims with descriptions, directions, travel tips, and photographs worth ten million words. Besides guiding you through Sedona, the book escorts you on day or overnight trips to Oak Creek Canyon, ruins of ancient dwelling sites, Jerome, Cottonwood and other parts of the Verde Valley, the Grand Canyon, Mogollon Rim, and Navajoland.

Just as important as guiding you, this book explores ways in which you can connect emotionally and spiritually with Sedona.

The alluring Sedona and red rock country, tucked in a colorful, geologic wonderland below the Mogollon Rim, beckon us with an encyclopedic array of enticements:

Rock formations resembling a cathedral, bell, or coffee pot.

Colors — salmon, beige, rust, violet, green, and black — that intensify or mellow as the sun and clouds float overhead.

Active recreation such as hiking, bicycle riding, and fishing.

Shopping in unique settings.

Art galleries displaying an eclectic variety of work by Sedona-based and other artists.

Vortexes that for New Agers store and release spiritual energy.

And so much more.

Sedona Calling's author, Lawrence W. Cheek, is a long-time Arizona Highways contributor. He wrote Scenic Sedona, first published by Arizona Highways in 1989. From 1990 to 1995, he had one of the best jobs in Arizona: Sedona "bureau chief" for Phoenix's Valley Guide Quarterly, a role requiring him to visit Sedona several times a year to research stories. He now lives in the Cascade foothills just east of Seattle, Washington.

In Sedona Calling, Cheek explores ways that you can connect with the extravagant landscape, from hiking to photography to meditation. He writes about how the land and its history influence artists, and how visitors can best go "gallery cruising." His treatment of art includes visual and performing arts and architecture.

Concluding his first chapter, Paradise Found, Cheek writes, ". . . Sedona today is a place of more variety than ever. There's intellectual capital, creative energy, remarkable sophistication, and . . . solitude."

–Bob Albano

BOOK DESIGN BARBARA DENNEY
PICTURE EDITOR RICHARD MAACK
MAPS KEVIN KIBSEY
COPY EDITORS STEVE FOX AND EVELYN HOWELL
BOOK EDITOR BOB ALBANO

Prepared by the Book Division of Arizona Highways magazine, a monthly publication of the Arizona Department of Transportation.

Publisher Nina M. La France
Managing Editor Bob Albano
Associate Editor Evelyn Howell
Art Director Mary Winkleman Velgos
Photography Director Peter Ensenberger
Research Editor Jeb Stuart Rosebrook
Production Director Cindy Mackey
Production Assistant Ellen Straine

Library of Congress Catalog Number 98-87498
ISBN 0-916179-81-8

Flagstaff

40

89A

89

Oak Creek

Verde River

Sedona

17

Jerome

89A

179

Camp Verde

Prescott

17

260

Trailheads

1. West Fork
2. A.B. Young
3. Sterling Pass
4. Lost Canyon
5. Boynton Canyon
6. Fay Canyon
7. Seven Sacred Pools
8. Cathedral Rock
9. Little Horse
10. Bell Rock

West Fork Oak Creek

Oak Creek

89A

1

OAK CREEK CANYON

2

SLIDE ROCK
STATE PARK

Sterling Pass 3

RED ROCK
SECRET MOUNTAIN
WILDERNESS

Boynton Canyon

Fay Canyon

FR 152

4

5

6

Boynton Pass Rd.

89A

Coffee Pot
Rock

Capitol
Butte

7

Soldier Pass Rd.

Dry Creek Road

To I-17

Schnebly Hill Road

Sedona

Dry Creek

Oak Creek

MUNDS MOUNTAIN
WILDERNESS

89A

Red Rock Loop Rd.

8

9

Cathedral
Rock

179

RED ROCK
STATE PARK

Verde Valley School Road

Bell
Rock

Courthouse
Butte

10

Oak Creek

Page
Springs

Village of
Oak Creek

COCONINO NATIONAL FOREST

Paradise Found

Origins of Red Rock Fever

This very diversity of climate and water supply which made these hills and plains a treasure house of wealth and beauty likewise made them a fragile dwelling for the modern white man. The engines wherewith he conquers these rocks and rills and templed hills are stronger than his understanding of what hills are, and more powerful than his vaunted love for them.

—ALDO LEOPOLD
From the unpublished book,
Southwest Game Fields

Top: A cliff dwelling occupies a niche in Lost Canyon. See Page 56. Larry Lindahl
Above: Sugarloaf Mountain, the low mound, and Coffee Pot Rock preside in this view of west Sedona. Bob & Suzanne Clemenz
Right: Cathedral Rock overlooks Oak Creek at Red Rock Crossing. George Stocking

They call it Red Rock Fever, and not as a joke. It begins as an eerie electric shiver near the apex of the spine and then migrates upward to the cortex, where it shuts down the Rational Judgment Department and blossoms into an irresistible urge to drop everything and move here. This progression may occur within a few hours of the victim's first sight of Sedona, or it may happen gradually, over years.

A New York stockbroker flew out for a vacation in 1973 and bought a house the next day. I asked him, wasn't that impulsive?

"Impulsive would be the same day," he replied.

Right: Globemallow, larkspur, paintbrush, and prickly pear cactus pave the base of Courthouse Rock. Larry Lindahl

A young South African with a degree in urban planning was hitchhiking around the States in 1986 when he came across Sedona. A quick look around confirmed for him that the settlement sorely needed urban planning, but since it wasn't yet incorporated, there wasn't much of it going on.

"So I waltzed into one of the Jeep tour companies and said, 'I'm a hell of a tour guide.' " They hired him.

I asked a sales clerk in an uptown boutique what had brought her here.

"God," she replied dreamily.

God, however, had not provided a way for her to actually live in Sedona on $6.50 an hour, so she was commuting from Camp Verde, 30 miles away and well out of sight of any red rocks.

"A lot of gallery owners are commuting these days, too," she said. In 1997, the median selling price of a house in Sedona was $285,000.

This is heart-stopping, achingly beautiful, ineffably alluring land. It should have been roped off as a national park back around the time of Teddy Roosevelt, saving it from the desultory development that even many resident Sedonans lament today. In a perfect world, no architecture would perturb the spectacle; no rumble of traffic would diminish the delicate tinkle of Oak Creek. But even

with all the development, the power of the place seems little diminished. About 3.5 million people come to visit every year, and more than a few of them find a way to stay.

Pretty amazing for a place whose prime attraction is rust.

The geology of Sedona looks complicated, but it can be explained simply in a few sentences:

Imagine a warm, shallow tropical sea. Sediment filtering through the water becomes the limestone base of the formations on Sedona's skyline today. The sea retreats, sandy desert usurps its place, and then the water laps up again. This cycle, begun 300 million years ago, keeps repeating, leaving limestone and sandstone strata of different colors and textures, which geologists can read in the rocks today. The spectacular spectrum of buff, orange, salmon, and vermilion in these strata — the Supai group, the

Hermit formation, and the Schnebly Hill formation — is the product of iron in the sandstone and limestone. When it rains, the iron rusts. The strange shapes of the rocks are due to the fact that each stratum, having a different degree of hardness, yields in a different way to the eroding forces of water, ice, and wind.

Paleontologists (and amateur fossil finders) also like the history of life embedded in the rocks. The Kaibab formation, a remnant of one of the oceans, yields fossils of sponges, crustaceans, and aquatic worms.

Thus goes the science, but the facts hardly explain the effect that this landscape has on the human spirit and emotion. People experience a complicated reaction to the landforms, the light, the weather, and the imagination.

The land that cradles Sedona is too botanically

luxurious to qualify as a desert — it enjoys an annual average rainfall of 17.22 inches — but it's also too open, too brittle, too aggressive to be forest. Try beating a straight path between any two points in the Sedona outback, and a motley militia of shindagger agave, prickly pear cactus, and catclaw acacia will cheerfully demonstrate its armament. Where rain congregates in the canyons, however, genuine forests do flourish — even if they're just six feet high and composed mainly of manzanita, a strange and beautiful bush-tree with spider limbs and satiny, wine-red bark. Variety is never a problem here; within 10 miles of town you can find seven distinct biological communities, ranging from desert grassland to Verde River riparian to ponderosa pine-fir forest on the overlooks of Oak Creek Canyon.

The red rocks, too, are alive. Not biologically, but, for want of a more tightly defined word, spiritually. They change in color and character every hour. I have seen them in a gray, woolly fog where they seemed to float, like ghostly icebergs cruising the sky. Under a bright midmorning sun, they may be a pale, cool violet; then as the day burns on, they shift into the red and orange regions of the spectrum. Approaching a late summer sunset, thunderclouds will sometimes roll in, turning

Below: At sunset, the rocks catch fire, and the landscape seems to guard secrets.
George Stocking

the sky to charcoal and enveloping the land in ominous shadow. Then there will be a slit in the overcast, and an arrow of amber sunlight will slash through and set one rock dramatically afire. At sunset on clear evenings, the fire colors turn to dying embers and then to rusty nuggets against a violet sky, and the draws and crevices blacken into voids that seem to guard inexpressible secrets.

Even as the rocks cycle through their chameleon moods, they remain immutable fixtures of the landscape. They seem to have existed forever and promise to persevere long after the momentary blight of civilization has passed. Sedona, more than any other place, recalls the English novelist J.B. Priestly's haunting description of Arizona: "It seemed to me the oldest country I had ever seen, the real antique land, first cousin to the moon."

The great Supreme Court justice and avid mountain man William O. Douglas explained simply and eloquently why we are drawn to such places.

"One has the sensation of being part of something much bigger than himself," he wrote in a book about his cherished North Cascades, "something great and majestic and wholesome."

SEDONA WAS FOUNDED IN 1902, a decade before President William Howard Taft, after some grumbling about the populist tilt of the territory's proposed

Previous spread: A winter storm casts a ghostly tone over Steamboat Rock. Randy Prentice
Top: With a little imagination, perhaps you can see why this rock is called Lion and Lioness. Dick Canby
Right: At the top of this Wilson Mountain trail, the hiker will find a fantastic view of Oak Creek Canyon. Mike Padian
Bottom: At 5,000 feet, the Sedona area rarely receives this much snow. The storm dropped five inches, frosting the sandstone cliffs and the piñon of the Soldier Pass area. Bob & Suzanne Clemenz

Left: Pendley Arch, or Window Rock, lies in Oak Creek Canyon.
Larry Lindahl
Below: Sterling Pass Trail leads through a forest.
Larry Lindahl
Bottom: Hiking along the West Fork of Oak Creek means getting your feet wet.
Bob & Suzanne Clemenz

constitution, signed Arizona into the family of states. Aside from a handful of homesteads in Oak Creek Canyon, the red rock country was wild, remote, and virtually unknown. But so was most of Arizona. Phoenix — the territorial capital and, in the imagination of one booster, her "commercial metropolis" — had a population of 5,500.

Sedona's story begins with two brothers, T.C. and Ellsworth Schnebly, who owned a hardware store in Gorin, Missouri. Ellsworth decided to test the Oak Creek area to see if the dry, mild climate would improve his health. It did, and he also fell in love with the land. The hardware store, meanwhile, wasn't thriving, so in 1902, T.C., his 25-year-old wife, and their two children followed, claiming an 80-acre homestead on the west bank of Oak Creek. They built a plain, two-story wood frame home with, of all things, a white picket fence, where Los Abrigados Resort sprawls today. They planted orchards, took in overnight guests, and applied for a post office permit. T.C. proposed two names for the settlement, both of which the postmaster rejected because they were too long to fit on a cancellation stamp. Ellsworth then suggested naming the settlement after T.C.'s wife, Sedona. Let us give thanks. T.C.'s ideas for a name had been Oak Creek Crossing and Schnebly Station.

Sedona Schnebly proved to be a woman who deserved the honor. She had been born into

a well-to-do family and had
grown up expecting to lead a
life of "big hats and
temperance meetings," said
her great-granddaughter, Lisa
Schnebly Heidinger. When
Sedona and T.C. left Missouri
for their Arizona adventure, it
infuriated Sedona's father to
the extent that he slashed her
out of his will.

"I think the move shocked
the hell out of her," Heidinger
said. "But she didn't realize
the extent of her own strength.
I have a feeling she wanted the
adventure, but never knew it
until she experienced it. She
tested very, very well."

Sedona, the accidental
pioneer, learned to tend the
orchards and herd cattle, ran a
primordial bed-and-breakfast
inn, played the piano to
entertain guests, killed
rattlesnakes with a broom,
eventually raised six children,
and watched helplessly as one
of them died in a tragic
accident. Her daughter Pearl
was riding a pony when she
spotted an Indian potsherd
and stopped to pick it up. The
pony spooked and bolted,
dragging Pearl alongside, her
foot caught in the stirrup.
Sedona raced after her, but
there was no way to stop the
battering. Sedona buried her
daughter in front of the house,
and withdrew into a cocoon of
remorse and nightmares.

Still, "She was a forerunner
of today's supermoms,"
Heidinger told me with pride.

An agave stalk stands watch on
the western edge of the Red Rock-
Secret Mountain Wilderness.
David H. Smith

In her grandma years, the locals came to call her Mother Schnebly, a warm tribute to the supermom of a town.

Visitors can contemplate Sedona Schnebly outside the city's public library today. The bronze sculpture by Susan Kliewer reconstructs her as bold and forthright, and as

Sedona and red rock formations unfold from an overlook along Schnebly Hill Road. George Stocking

graceful as possible within the swaddling confines of a Victorian dress. There is also a revealing photo of her in the archives. Her huge, impassive, doe eyes look like bottomless reservoirs of determination. She was not beautiful, but she had the right stuff to be a pioneer.

The first 50 years were uneventful for Sedona, the town. Oak Creek offered the only available water, and it wasn't enough for large-scale

agriculture or development. Government geologists insisted there was no water underground. In 1948, a driller who suspected differently sank a well, and it produced. That primed Sedona for its boom.

Page Stegner, a writer who went to a boarding school nearby, recalls the Sedona of 1951 as a rustic refueling station offering not much more than cold pop, gas, and cigarettes, the place "where they coined the phrase, 'If you

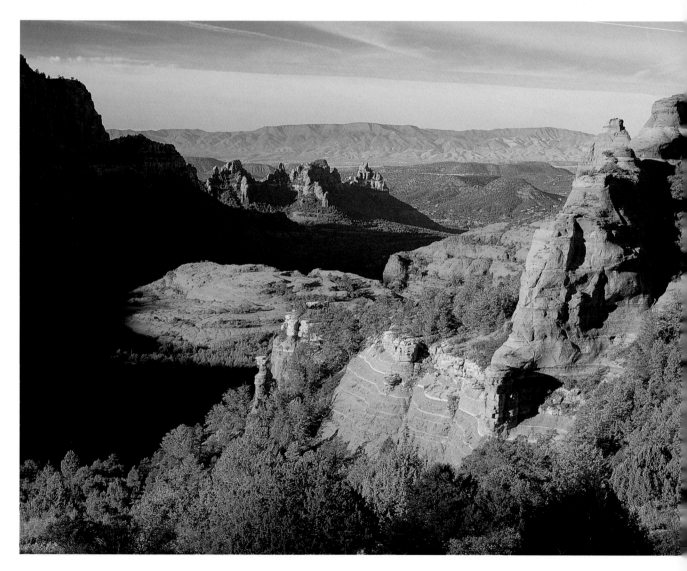

blink, you'll miss it.' "

In an otherwise cranky essay for *Audubon* magazine in 1981, Stegner remembered his happily misspent days in innocent Sedona, "when the sun would bake the valley to a brickyard, and the red dust would powder so fine that it clogged the pores and formed a little nosebleed rime around the nostrils, (and) I'd scuttle down through the washes like a scorpion shaken out of a hot boot, fling myself into one of the sandstone pools upstream from the ford, and cling there to a root snaggle below the surface until my head would ache behind the eyes from the cold."

When Stegner returned to Sedona 30 years later, he didn't much like what he saw — an unincorporated, sprawling town burgeoning in wealth and sophistication and clotting the desert air with powdery dust as contractors resculpted the red hills to make flat places for new shops and houses. What chance does this outpost of Eden stand, he wondered, "when one out of every 20 residents is a real estate agent?"

That figure, of course, was gross exaggeration. I researched a magazine story on Sedona the year after Stegner's essay and counted. Just one in 38 residents was a real estate agent.

Most Sedonans today lament the frenzy of the boom and the vacuum of coherent planning in which it occurred. Since Sedona had no town government of its own and it straddled a county line,

Sedona and T.C. Schnebly pose in 1897, five years before homesteading on Oak Creek. Special Collections Library, Northern Arizona University, Flagstaff

residents lurched from one county seat to the other in an endless succession of zoning and development fights. The real issue — how to accommodate growth without scarring the scenery that people were coming to see — was too thorny for such a haphazard process to grasp. The opportunity to create a special kind of community was lost. Sedona today has no definable town center, public park, nor arts district. There's no public access to Oak Creek as it meanders through the middle of town — one of the prettiest places in all of Arizona, forbidden by a phalanx of NO TRESPASSING signs.

Belatedly, planning took root in Sedona in the 1990s. Piece by piece, the newly incorporated city adopted a sign ordinance, a community plan, and architectural design review to try to preserve the scenic views and discourage buildings that leap out of the rocks and clamor for attention. None of this was easy.

"The community started off really polarized," recalled Roger Eastman, a city planner. "But we all had the same goal — to integrate the built forms of the town into the natural forms around us. By the time we were finished, both sides had come around to the middle — a kind of a greening of the developers and a browning of the environmentalists."

Richard V. Dahl, a prominent real estate agent, expressed a sentiment that you didn't hear much in the Sedona of 20 years back.

"Living here carries with it a responsibility," he told me in a 1997 conversation. "We live in one of the most treasured sites in the world. It's not our private preserve."

The planning is making some difference. The McDonald's in west Sedona sports teal, not golden, arches. A car wash melts into the red rock background with a low profile and a salmon color scheme. A big three-level Best Western motel steps down a hillside like an angular Slinky, instead of presenting a hulking three-story facade to the street. At the same time, though, Sedona's increasing wealth has meant the building of bigger and bigger custom homes on prominent hillsides — 5,000 to 10,000 square feet is not uncommon — and nothing in the native repertoire of runt trees grows high enough to hide them.

By 1999, the settlement had grown into a sophisticated, small city of 9,800 people. Based on

Sedona's development regulations, planners say the city will stretch to about 17,000 before it presses against the last national forest boundary. Nobody seems sorry that the gate is scheduled to be closed — at least not yet.

FALLING FOR THE ROCKS — and the color, the crisp starlight, even the botanical cutlery — is quick and inevitable. It may take two or three visits to appreciate the quirks and traditions of Sedona's peculiar stew of civilization, but it happens. Where else could you enjoy a white-tablecloth resort breakfast of an orange frittata with a cloud of tomatillo salsa — precisely the colors of the canyon outside — followed by a visit to a psychic who advertises herself as a "multidimensional glitch remover," and then rattle away in a gaily colored Jeep to tour prehistoric ruins and male or female (your choice) vortexes?

For a couple of generations before the boom of the '70s (and the '80s and '90s), Sedona remained a sleepy hangout for a few artists, a sprinkling of midcentury pioneers, and second-home owners enjoying an escape from Phoenix or southern California. People discovered it through word of mouth, travel writers, and exposure on the silver screen.

The movie industry discovered Sedona before the tourists, beginning in 1923 with Victor Fleming's direction of the silent-movie adaptation of Zane Grey's novel, *The Call*

of the Canyon. Although for a long time the red rocks were just black and white, the visual drama of wide, open spaces, towering buttes, and exotic chaparral formed a perfect stage set for classic Westerns: Where in North America could a man on a horse gallop around a land more evocative of heroic challenge? (And yet Hollywood still itched to improve it. In the 1950 Jimmy Stewart blockbuster *Broken Arrow*, fake plaster-of-paris saguaros were installed around the Sedona outback to suggest the iconic West more thoroughly. A saguaro would no sooner grow as a native plant in Sedona than in San Francisco.) After the Western genre burned out, Sedona continued as a backdrop for TV episodes, music videos, commercials, and print ads. The red rocks have helped sell Land Rovers, Kodak film, Lee jeans, Ray-Ban sunglasses, and, for reasons less clear, the services of 1st Alabama Bank.

The 1980s brought international sophistication — high-end restaurants, high-priced art in the galleries, and destination resorts. One resort, Enchantment, actually started out with a dress code — jackets at dinner, "traditional whites" on the tennis courts. Sedona Schnebly, who borrowed T.C.'s overalls for work, would not have understood. (Now under more enlightened management, Enchantment no longer dictates guests' dress.)

The '80s also brought spiritual seekers, mystics, cranks, and fanatics. And

especially entrepreneurs. The forms in which Sedona's mystique is marketed are as fanciful as the red rocks themselves. A few years ago, howling coyotes infested every boutique and gallery, in every conceivable form. Then the icon became Kokopelli, the prehistoric hunchback flute player. Sedona boutiques

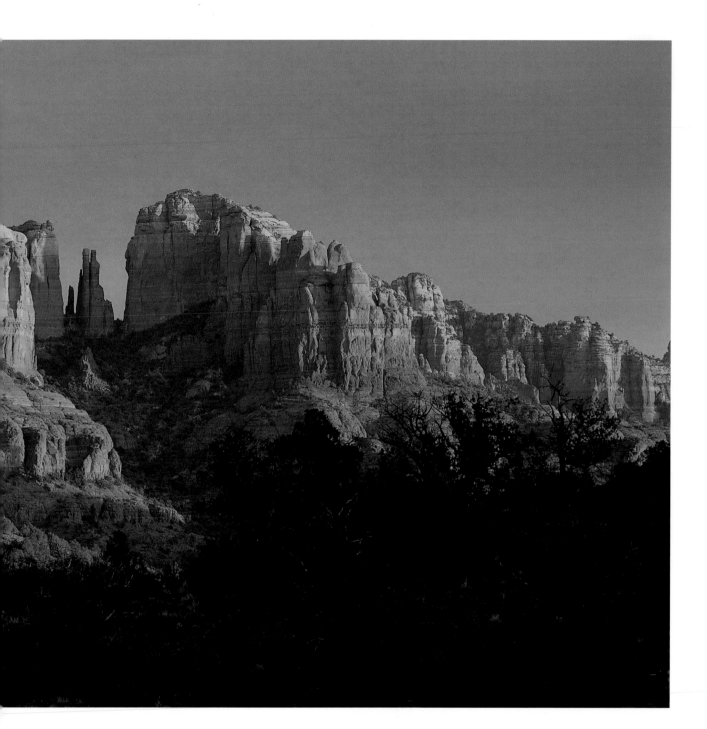

present him on T-shirts, electric switch plates, earrings, wind chimes, lawn sculptures, napkin holders, and boxes of Indian corn bread mix. The American West sometimes seems too huge, too deep, and too complicated to grasp unless we repackage it as a cartoon.

Sedona even markets its distinctive dirt — ready to wear. A local fashion company advertises shirts hand-dyed with Sedona Red Dirt — "Famous for its long-lasting properties, (it) has been blessed and is believed to bring good luck to the wearer."

For obvious reasons, Sedona has become a mecca for well-off retirees. But the

Cathedral Rock dominates the landscape seen from Red Rock Loop Road, west of Sedona.
Larry Lindahl

median age is now falling, thanks to the fax, the computer, and the Internet. There is a steadily growing community of freelance

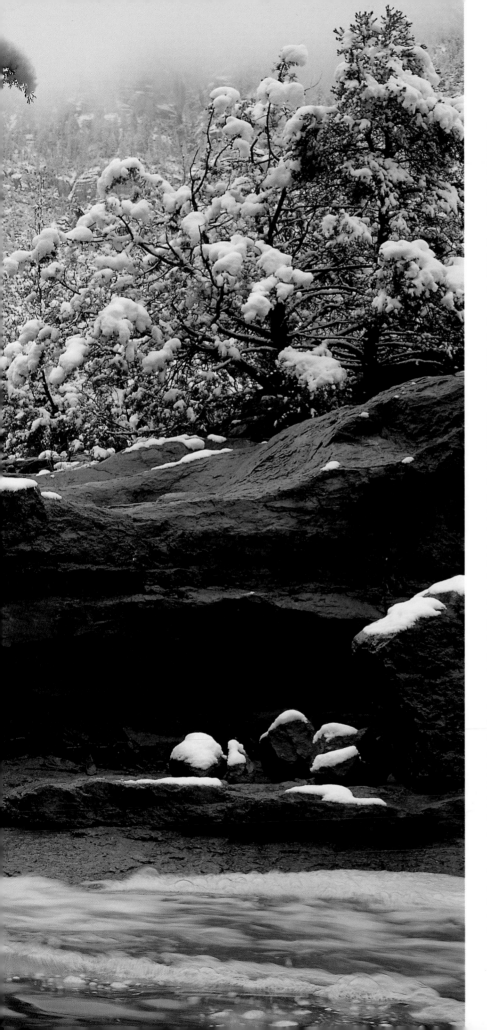

"consultants" who became allergic to the urban tumult of New York, San Francisco, or Phoenix, and who are now wiring into the world from Sedona.

Ed Southwell is one of the refugees. He didn't exactly catch Red Rock Fever; he just knew he wanted something other than city life.

"We wanted our eight-year-old daughter to have the same freedoms we had when we grew up," he said, "such as being able to ride her bike around the block in safety."

Southwell has run his national market research business from his Sedona home since 1992. There are a few disadvantages: a two-hour drive to the nearest major airport, and a relatively primitive communications web — "There's not even a local AOL phone number." But business is fine, and clients are envious. "They're always trying to come up with reasons to have meetings here. When I'm making a presentation, I'll throw in a slide of Sedona, and someone will always say, 'Oh, wow, that is such a cool place.'"

Richard Drayton is another. In the 1980s, he abandoned a prosperous commercial art career in Los Angeles to live in Sedona and paint. Then came the digital revolution, and he invented a prosperous commercial art career in Sedona, creating artwork on the computer and

The Sedona area is too wet to be a desert, as shown by this Bear Wallow Canyon scene along Schnebly Hill Road. Lurking in the fog is the Mogollon Rim. Larry Lindahl sending it by modem to clients around the country.

"My studio looks more and more like a computer room than an art studio," he said. "I keep a stack of colored pencils on a desk so I can look at them once in a while and remind myself of what I am."

The consequence of all this is that Sedona today is a place of more variety than ever. There's intellectual capital, creative energy, remarkable sophistication, and, with somewhat more effort than it once took, solitude. If you come to hike, more than 100 trails lace the surrounding red rocks and canyons. If you want to buy art, Sedona's 50-odd galleries now exhibit everything from reproductions of prehistoric pottery to incomprehensible abstract sculpture. If you just want to observe the interaction between modern *Homo sapiens* and a landscape that ought to humble us, but often doesn't, Sedona is the perfect stage set.

I still can't help mourning the Sedona that never was — Sedona National Park, 100 square miles of red hills and mountains and canyons that nothing except nature would ever get to tinker with. My spine, which is stuffed with populist marrow, stiffens with the principle that a place of such profound beauty should be equally accessible — and equally inaccessible — to all. But my cortex blooms with hypocrisy. I ache with Red Rock Fever. If I could afford it, I would move here, too.

Dense vegetation lines Oak Creek near Midgely Bridge.
Larry Lindahl

When You Go

With an elevation of 4,300 feet, Sedona enjoys four distinct seasons, none too extreme. June, July, and August, however, routinely bring highs in the 90s. Midsummer nights, happily, sink to the 50s and 60s. Sedona entertains the most people during its mildest seasons: March through May and September through October. On weekends in these months, getting a room without a reservation may be impossible. Least crowded: the first two weeks of December and all of January.

Recommendation: Visit Sedona when the fewest people are visiting Sedona. Late fall and winter are lovely, and the occasional threat of rain, fog, or snow only enhances the experience — the red rocks become unpredictably different characters in the wet. The only disadvantages to a winter visit are the shorter days, which shrink the possibilities for outdoor activities, and the fact that some lodges in Oak Creek Canyon close for the season.

Sedona-area accommodations include forest campsites maintained by the Forest Service (see pages 50 and 59), private RV parks, motels, B&Bs, rustic cabins in Oak Creek Canyon, and world-class resorts. Timeshare condos are increasingly popular. For any of these, make reservations as far in advance as possible. The Sedona-Oak Creek Canyon Chamber of Commerce is very helpful; call (520) 282-7722 for assistance with lodging or a free information packet.

If Sedona is full, stay in Cottonwood, 20 miles southwest on State Route 89A; or in Flagstaff, 30 miles north on State Route 89A. The Cottonwood-Verde Valley Chamber of Commerce phone number is (520) 634-7593. Flagstaff tourist information is (520) 774-9541 or (800) 842-7293.

The Internet is blooming with information on Sedona. A Yahoo! search with the word "Sedona" turned up more than 100 Web sites, from print-them-out-yourself Forest Service booklets to an omnium-gatherum of New Age mystica. Some useful Web addresses are:

http://www.arizonaguide.com/sedona (Sedona-Oak Creek Canyon Chamber of Commerce).
http://www.city.sedona.net/ (City of Sedona).
http://www.sedona.net (provides links to sites covering lodging, activities, and a chat room).
http://bb.sedona.net (bed-&-breakfast inns)

A good way to get a sense of the community is with a mail subscription to its twice-weekly newspaper, the *Sedona Red Rock News*, (520) 282-7795, or the quarterly *Sedona Magazine*, (520) 282-9022. Visitors from distant states or foreign countries generally fly into Phoenix Sky Harbor, the nearest major airport, and rent a car for the drive to Sedona, which takes about two hours. There is no regularly scheduled commercial passenger service to the Sedona Airport, which serves light aircraft with a 5,100-foot paved and lighted runway. (520) 282-4487.

The nearly universal mistake in visiting Sedona is squeezing the trip into too short a time. This is not chamber-of-commerce prattle; it's an observation from dozens of visits. Five to seven days is ideal. This allows one or two excursions to attractions such as the Grand Canyon, Jerome, or the Navajo Reservation (see chapters 4 and 5), and enough time in the cradle of the red rocks to get a sense of the place.

Month	Average maximum (°F)	Average minimum (°F)	Average precipitation (inches)
January	55	30	1.70
February	59	32	1.54
March	63	35	1.67
April	72	42	1.17
May	81	49	0.56
June	91	57	0.49
July	95	65	1.89
August	92	64	2.42
September	88	58	1.51
October	78	49	1.16
November	65	37	1.32
December	56	31	1.79

Inside Sedona

The Arts Flourish

Tlaquepaque re-creates the
architecture and culture of
an 18th-century Spanish
Colonial village.
Top: Luminarias light the
way at Christmas. Tom Bean
Above: Folk dancing
traditions continue.
Bob & Suzanne Clemenz

Opposite: West Sedona
homes and businesses dot
the landscape between
west Sedona rock
formations, including
Coffee Pot Rock in the
background, and Airport
Mesa. George Stocking

*All great art is the work
of the whole living creature,
body and soul, and chiefly
of the soul.*

— JOHN RUSKIN
19th-century English art critic

Not for the first time,
Sedona artist Richard
Drayton has painted the red
rocks almost without using red
paint. The craggy buttes on the
canvas before us reveal a
spectrum of possibly 50 shades
of cream, peach, gold, orange,
blue, magenta, purple, and
indigo. But the only red is a
tingling, luminescent hairline
border on the rocks separating
sunlight from shadow, and it's so
subtle he has to point it out
before I see it.

From this description, you'd
expect Drayton's portraits of the
Sedona landscape to be quirky
and personal interpretations,
but you'd be wrong. They are
startlingly realistic. In fact, his
redless paintings appear to
capture more of the reality of
the red rocks than the work of
most painters.

Drayton smiles, absorbing
pleasure in the compliment.

"It's taken me 10 years of
painting the landscape to get to
this point," he says.

Gallery owner Jim Ratliff

Los Abrigados Resort strings out 350,000 lights to create man-made splendor.
Bob & Suzanne Clemenz

understands what Drayton discovered: "So many artists come here to paint the red rocks because they're enamored with the color, and they fail miserably. The paintings turn out flat. The reason is that they're missing the point. The red rocks aren't about color; they're about light."

True enough. But Sedona artists will tell you that their great rock garden is about much more. They will say it's about mystery, inspiration, obsession. About ineffable colors that glow in the mind even though they will not register on Kodachrome. About the power this landscape has to transform an artist's vision, temperament, and way of seeing the world. And ultimately about the soul.

The Visual Arts

The red rocks have been luring artists to Sedona for more than half a century. Max Ernst, the German surrealist, built a place here in the 1940s and declared to his friends, "There are only two places in the world I want to live — Paris and Sedona." In 1961, the Egyptian-born sculptor Nassan Gobran and a few volunteers founded the Sedona Art Center, which continues today as a nonprofit art school, gallery, and community theater. In 1963, Western artist Joe Beeler sat down at a table in the Oak Creek Tavern with three friends — Charlie Dye, John Hampton, and George Phippen — and

formed the Cowboy Artists of America. Sedona used to major in cowboys, Indian jewelry, and Western landscapes, but it has spread out and grown up, becoming more eclectic and sophisticated. By 1999, some 300 artists were living and working in Sedona and about 50 galleries were spanning a wide range of price, genre, and taste.

What draws artists to Sedona? Most are not here to paint the red rocks. They all are inspired by the place, but it works on them in different ways.

D. Michael McCarthy cheerfully labels himself a throwback, a 19th-century Hudson River School painter time-warped into the modern world through some insidious trick of fate. His paintings contemplate romanticized, mystical mountains and heroic canyons of impossible proportions. His landscapes do not, could not exist. But to anyone who knows Sedona, the pristine, iridescent light in them triggers the sense of déjà vu.

"Light really is the prime mover in my painting, and I've never lived anywhere else that had such a dramatic influence on my perception of it," he says. "I'm interested in the larger workings of nature, the interactions of sky and earth, and this is where you can see it the most dramatically. The colors in this landscape are pretty harsh, and yet the light does wonderful things to them. For example, when rain is falling over the rim of a butte and there's a rainbow overhead, everything is muted. A lot of times I'll put an Arizona sky into a painting of someplace else."

27

Mike Medow is a sculptor and painter whose art focuses exclusively on the human form — females, to be precise, whose bodies are exaggerated and distorted for their fluidity of line, not overt sexuality. He carves his sculptures in native alligator juniper, always a twisted, gnarled, unpredictable wood, working with chisels and rasps, never planning in advance but allowing the wood to yield up the form that nature locked within it.

The light and landforms haven't affected his art, he says, but his introspective Sedona lifestyle has.

"There's not much for an adult to do here, after hiking," he says in an observation that will furrow brows over at the Chamber of Commerce, "so maybe it gives me more drive to stay busy. I'm forced to go deep within."

Sedona photographer Lou DeSerio makes his living portraying the surrounding landscape in the most literal way possible — big Cibachrome prints that render the extravagant colors and forms in minute detail. But it isn't just about surfaces for him, either.

"I like to think that this place produces a deeper look into oneself," he told me in a 1991 conversation. "Sedona provides an environment where I can hear myself better, where I can connect, where I can evolve."

Taking a devil's advocate role, I asked DeSerio whether such a lovely, peaceful environment might not be detrimental to an artist's evolution. A lot of great art, I argued, arises out of tension and conflict.

"Conflict helps in self-development," he agreed. "But a lot of energy is taken up in seeking resolution, and then all that is subtracted from your art. And if you find yourself in conflict after conflict, then you get stuck in it, and you stagnate."

DeSerio's thinking connected perfectly in 1980s Sedona. In *Scenic Sedona*, published by *Arizona Highways* in 1989, I observed that for all the diversity and quality of the art being created and sold in Sedona, none of it was combative or controversial, or even eccentric. Ratliff, the gallery owner, offered a theory that seemed, at the time,

certainly intriguing and maybe correct. There is an energy in the red rocks, he said; he didn't know what it is, but somehow it fuels the creative process.

"But it can only be used in a

Top: A bronze of Merlin by John M. Soderberg is juxtaposed with red rock country. Bob & Suzanne Clemenz
Above: This photograph by D. Michael McCarthy of his painting of Oak Creek Canyon shows his infusion of mystical qualities into his work.

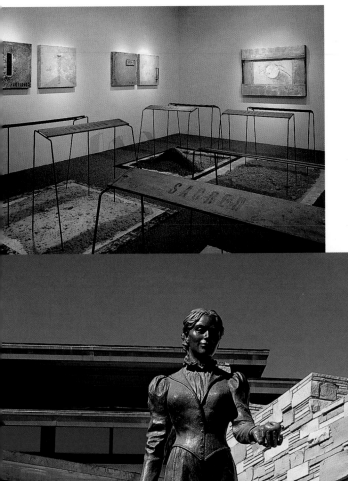

Left: Karen Licher's installation at the Select Art Gallery reflects Sedona's artistic eclecticism. Richard Maack
Below: Sedona sculptor Susan Kliewer's bronze of Sedona Schnebly stands in front of the Sedona Public Library. Bob & Suzanne Clemenz

positive way," he said. "If people try to use that energy to create something negative, they don't stay around. The red rocks spit them right out of here."

But Sedona has changed, even as that red rock energy surely springs eternal. There is no sudden eruption of "negative" art in Sedona, but there is an influx of new people and new ideas, a growing national and international clientele, and with all that, some art that provokes controversy. Which is healthy.

Fuller Barnes, a talented and imaginative scrap-metal sculptor who moved to Sedona in 1992, fabricated a jagged dragon out of rusty car and tractor parts and parked it in front of a real estate brokerage in town. People called, scolding the office for displaying the image of Satan. The complaint was relayed to Barnes, who was ecstatic.

"Well, great!" he exclaimed. "Now we know what he looks like."

Bruce Tobias opened The Select Art Gallery in 1995 to dire predictions.

"If there were a demand for an urban-style contemporary art gallery," people told him, "it would already be here."

He ignored them and opened a gallery that welcomed combative and controversial art, up to and including live nude body painting. Sales doubled in the second year.

"We push the (Sedona) envelope," he said, "but that's expected of us now. You can't always be a sheep following the herd."

The best news for the Sedona art buyer today is that

29

the range of available work is wide and unpredictable. The variety now approaches Santa Fe's, which could not have been said 10 years ago. At least some of the artists are basking in Sedona's increasing wealth and sophistication. Fuller Barnes is making outdoor sculpture and furniture for Sedonans on commissions from $500 to $12,000. Usually his patrons trust his imagination.

"Mostly, the designs are left up to me," he said. "That's been terrific; I need that freedom."

The ominous development in Sedona is the escalating price of real estate, which is becoming a formidable barrier to artists newly seeking inspiration in the red rocks. The 300 working artists living in Sedona mostly bought in years back. Perhaps an artistic Darwinism may prevail. If only the most imaginative artists can figure out how to live in Sedona, then maybe we will see the most imaginative art.

Architecture

If it were being proposed today, the Chapel of the Holy Cross could not be built. There would be furious controversy and a flurry of lawsuits. Someone such as Robert McConnell, once dean of the University of Arizona College of Architecture, would be called to testify.

"The best thing we architects can do for the mountains," he would say, "is to stay away from them."

Stars of the Milky Way rise into a moonlit sky over the Chapel of the Holy Cross. Frank Zullo

Twenty years back, McConnell said precisely that to me in an interview, and I reflect on it every time I return to Sedona. Can a building ever enhance a mountain? Can architecture ever meld with nature so gracefully that it simply belongs?

Nearly always, a resounding No! But some of the Sinagua and Anasazi ruins of northern Arizona grow from their cliffside sites with such inevitability that they seem almost to invest the native rock with intelligence — as does the Chapel of the Holy Cross, Sedona's most inspired man-made landmark.

Marguerite Brunswig Staude, a Los Angeles sculptor born in 1899 to wealth and social prominence, had long been obsessed with the idea of a cathedral that would lead people to God through art —

contemporary art, not Gothic. In 1932, she attended a Lenten mass at St. Patrick's Cathedral in New York City and found herself thinking, as she later wrote, "How come the Church clings to its past glory while seeming totally to ignore the present, as though it did not exist?" She decided to commission her own cathedral. After World War II aborted a scheme for a Budapest site by

Tlaquepaque brings shopping to a
Spanish Colonial setting.
Left: Tulips and a fountain define a
courtyard. Bob & Suzanne Clemenz
Above: Shoppers inspect Native
American creations. Tom Bean

Frank Lloyd Wright, she
retained Anshen & Allen
Architects of San Francisco, and
together they selected this niche
in the red rocks. Instead of a
cathedral, it would be a small
but dramatic chapel dedicated
to the memory of her parents —
"A spiritual fortress," she wrote,
"so charged with God that it
spurs man's spirit Godward!"

A more godly site would
have been hard to find. The
chapel, built in 1955-56, seems
to thrust itself out of two
rounded sandstone knobs. Twin
Buttes thrusts vertically skyward
behind it, like the stage set of
some epic drama. The hillocks
immediately around are gruff
and angular and spiked with
ocotillo and agave.

Anshen & Allen wisely
decided not to try to upstage

this natural spectacle, but they
didn't hide their building in it,
either. The architecture is simple
to the point of austerity, which
was much in vogue in the 1950s,
but it is also confident and
assertive. Imagine a concrete-
aggregate cereal box with one
narrow side removed so the long
sides can splay outward, and a
great concrete cross, 90 feet
high, thrust through the center.
This is all there is. No splash of
color, no ornament, no
articulation to break up those
vast, flat walls. Inside, it is just
as severe. No stained glass, no
pipe organ. There are a handful
of contemporary sculptures by
Staude and others.

But it isn't a simple building.
It exudes as many moods as the
landscape around it. In the full
sun, it has a defiant attitude.

"These rocks around may
erode," it seems to say, "I will
not."

But as the late afternoon sun
fades and the rocks turn orange,
then deep rust, the building
retreats, absorbing the colors,

going gently into the good night
with the mountains. Then the
full moon comes out and frosts
the chapel in silver fire, and it
seems like the last citadel of
man standing alone in the
universe.

I stayed outside watching
the brittle moonlight finger the
chapel one night, and I was
transfixed. I thought back to a
conversation with another dean
of architecture, John Meunier of
Arizona State University.

"If a building is worthy of
contemplation, then it qualifies
as architecture," Meunier said.
"If it rewards that
contemplation, then it's
probably good architecture."
This chapel rewards by enriching
the human spirit. It is one of the
rare buildings that justifies its
intrusion in a glorious natural
setting.

Tlaquepaque (pronounced
"tlockay-pockay") likewise
could not be built as it is today.
Half of it lies in Oak Creek's
flood plain, and it crowds into
an environmentally sensitive
grove of 200-year-old Arizona
sycamores.

But things were looser in
1971 when Nevada hotel and
restaurant developer Abe Miller
began building Tlaquepaque,
named after an artists' colony in
Guadalajara, Mexico, and
modeled on an idealized 18th-
century Spanish Colonial village.
Miller originally planned to let
artists live and work upstairs
and sell their creations on the
ground floor, but the Sedona
art market of the '70s wasn't
spinning off enough money
to make that practical.
Boutiques, galleries, and

restaurants eventually occupied both levels of the village.

But Miller did not dilute the architecture of his dream. He loved Spanish Colonial Mexico and personally imported as much of it as he could to weave into Tlaquepaque: antique church doors, ornamental stone lintels, fountains, gates, bells, decorative wrought iron.

"He worked his tail off all his life," said his daughter, Marilyn Cordovano. "When he was finally in a position to be able to do Tlaquepaque, he was like a little kid in a candy store."

Miller also bowed to a historic treasure on the site: those hoary sycamores, their white trunks and branches poking and lurching in every direction. Any reasonable developer would have summoned the chain saws, first thing. But Miller envisioned the trees as an integral part of the architecture and braided the buildings around them. Branches writhe through passageways created especially for them, and verdant foliage embraces the arcades and towers. The trees tease the sunlight, breaking it up and making it benign. They harmonize so gracefully with the architecture that the whole development seems like one living organism.

Most of the modern attempts at Spanish Colonial revivalism in the Southwest are more like cartoons or clichés than real architecture. Tlaquepaque is unique in that it goes deeper and discovers the spirit of a different place and time, even though it

romanticizes the image. It exudes quiet dignity and provides intimate courtyards for relaxation or contemplation, qualities offered by few other shopping environments built in the late 20th century. Abe Miller, thankfully, was behind his time.

For a long time, Tlaquepaque and the chapel were the only buildings around town that took nothing away from the natural beauty around them. Lately, however, more and more private homes and public buildings are arising in harmony with — how else to say this? — the spirit of Sedona.

For example, drop into the Sedona Public Library, completed in 1995 by Design Group Architects, a small Sedona firm consisting of Mike Bower and Max Licher. Its form is based loosely on the historic apple-packing barns in Oak Creek Canyon, and its skin is a prehistoric Anasazi-like veneer of rough sandstone masonry, which automatically integrates the building into the colors and textures of the red rocks forming its backdrop. But like Drayton with his landscape paintings, Bower and Licher have spent enough time prowling the rocks to understand the great variations in their color — red, orange, pink, ocher, white, black. For the library, they actually ordered the stonemasons to use a prescribed percentage of each color of stone to build the walls.

"The more rock that we use," Licher says, "the more it could be a unifying element that

would give Sedona an architectural character of its own."

Enchantment Resort, designed by Phoenix architect George Christensen, is a praiseworthy lesson in humility. Its puebloesque casitas slip gracefully into the folds of Boynton Canyon northwest of town without any architectural fuss. And yet, when I hike in this favorite canyon, I can't help comparing it with the Sinagua cliff dwellings all around me: Without expert eyes, they can't be seen at all.

Performing Arts

Why should jazz be a creation of the night? What's so magical about a crowded, smoky Bourbon Street bar? Why not welcome it into the open and give it a sapphire sky, clean air, and room to breathe?

That was the idea behind Jazz on the Rocks, Sedona's annual jazz festival, founded in 1982 by local pianist Johnny Gilbert. A thousand enthusiasts showed up that first year. By 1985, attendance had more than doubled, and the festival board decided they could shoot for the stars. Since then, the list of headliners at Jazz on the Rocks reads like a who's who of jazz: the Count Basie Orchestra, Nancy Wilson, Diane Schuur, Dizzy Gillespie, Tuck and Patti. Five thousand tickets now sell for each festival.

The performing arts are

Right: Enchantment Resort fits without fanfare into Boynton Canyon, like a modern-day pueblo. Tom Johnson

growing up quickly in Sedona. It's still a small city, so it has to import much of its talent, but the audiences are hungry. The Sedona Chamber Music Society brings in a dozen classical ensembles every year. The Sedona Art Center stages community theater productions, and director Craig Thompson hopes to bring in professional actors to work alongside the amateurs. Work is proceeding on a $9-million, 50-acre Sedona Cultural Park in west Sedona, which will become the permanent venue for Jazz on the Rocks and other arts organizations.

Can the red rocks inspire and nourish the performing arts, as they have painting and sculpture? Some years ago, Jazz on the Rocks booked the great jazz drummer Louis Bellson and his

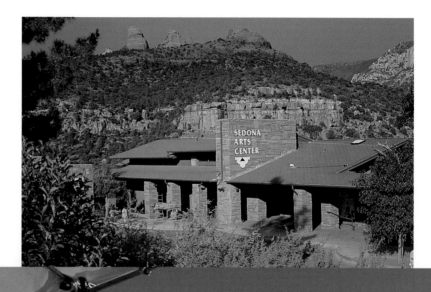

Performing arts come clean in Sedona: Below: The Jazz on the Rocks festival. Right: Sedona Arts Center. Both by Bob & Suzanne Clemenz

wife, the legendary Pearl Bailey. She fell ill, but Bellson came anyway. He strolled the festival grounds, his eyes feasting, and said, "If Pearly was here, she would say, 'God lives here.' "

A few years later, blues singer Doug MacLeod recalled his first gig at Jazz on the Rocks for *Arizona Highways*: "I remember standing on the stage, red rocks off to my left, red rocks off to my right. And a thought hit me: It's impossible to do a bad show in this place."

When You Go

Gallery cruising in Sedona can be exhilarating and exhausting. There are more than any reasonable human would want to visit in a week, and no published guide lists all the galleries with their current specialties. Fortunately, most of the galleries are sprinkled around town in three clusters: Along State Route 179 within a mile or so of the "Y" junction, in Tlaquepaque, and around uptown Sedona. Others are loosely scattered along State Route 89A in west Sedona. Art enthusiasts will also find day trips to Flagstaff and Jerome to be useful.

As more and more galleries open — and the number grew from about 30 to 50 between 1988 and 1999 — they increasingly specialize. Personal taste will suggest where you look. Specialties include Western, Southwestern/Native American, photography, landscape, whimsical contemporary, provocative contemporary, and New Age. Several galleries are eclectic and unpredictable.

Carry a notebook to help remind you where and what you saw that you liked. It is no breach of gallery etiquette to make a lower offer on a higher-priced piece, but it is unethical to try an end run by contacting the artist directly. Advice on buying prehistoric Indian artifacts: don't. Counterfeits and illegally obtained pieces abound. Contemporary pottery and legitimate reproductions are much better reminders of your northern Arizona experience.

The most important tip for anyone who wants to attend any of the festivals in Sedona is: Plan ahead, way ahead. Tickets sell out, rooms fill up. Six months ahead is not too early to book a room for Jazz on the Rocks.

The Sedona-Oak Creek Canyon Chamber of Commerce, (520) 282-7722, each year compiles a free calendar of events, which is a good place to start planning. Here are some of the arts events and festivals:

March: Sedona International Film Festival. An annual weekend of morning-to-midnight screenings of independent, foreign, and documentary films. (520) 282-0747.

May: Western Americana Festival. (520) 282-9441.

May-June: Sedona Chamber Music Festival. (520) 526-2256.

July-August: Flagstaff Festival of the Arts, a month-long music festival centered at Northern Arizona University. Classical, pops, and ethnic music and dance. (800) 266-7740 or (520) 774-7750.

September: Jazz on the Rocks. (520) 282-1985. Tickets go on sale May 1. The huge outdoor Saturday show may not sell out, but the intimate headliner concert Friday night definitely will. Bring hat, sunblock, and folding stadium or beach seat. Maximum allowable seat back height is 30 inches.

October: Sculpture Walk at Los Abrigados, sponsored by the Sedona Arts Center. (520) 282-3809.

October: Sedona Arts Festival, a juried show with works of more than 125 artists from around the country. (520) 204-9456.

Thanksgiving-January: Red Rock Fantasy of Lights at Los Abrigados. Sedona families deck the walls, trees, and lawns of the 22-acre resort property with holiday displays incorporating more than a million lights. (520) 282-1777.

The Chapel of the Holy Cross is open 9 A.M. to 5 P.M. daily. There is no Mass, but lay leaders from St. John Vianney Catholic Church conduct a prayer service open to the public every Monday at 5 P.M. (except during the winter).

SEDONA IN SPIRIT

*Something deeply hidden
had to be behind things.*

— ALBERT EINSTEIN

*From a hand-written
autobiographical note*

No scenic attraction or environmental issue, ironically, has won Sedona as much international publicity — some of it, say the locals, unwanted — as the "vortexes." Is there some physical or metaphysical energy in the red rocks? How do these spiritual hot spots actually work? How does Sedona, with its soaring cost of living, keep attracting psychics and New Age entrepreneurs who haven't exactly lived a life of stock options?

Whatever one's feelings about geographical spirituality, it's big here. A Northern Arizona University study in 1996 found that 64 percent of visitors were seeking some form of spiritual experience in Sedona. Of those, 43 percent specifically mentioned the vortexes.

The New Age arrived in Sedona in the early 1980s, as a few believers declared it one of the planet's "power points" — a place where an indefinable form of energy flowed freely out of the earth. Page Bryant, a self-proclaimed psychic, identified four concentrations, or "vortexes," of this energy within a few miles of town. Someone noted that the very name of the town appeared to be an electromagnetic omen: Sedona spelled backwards becomes Anodes, the plates in vacuum tubes that attract electrons.

In August, 1987, Sedona attracted 5,000 people — true believers and the merely curious — to the Harmonic Convergence, a planet-healing festival. At sunrise on Airport Mesa, one of the "vortexes," they formed circles of 12 people, chanted the Om mantra, raised their left arms to the sky and pointed their right arms downward to direct positive energy into the earth. Some directed their aspirations toward the stars, buying $150 tickets to sit on Bell Rock at the moment it was supposed to depart for the galaxy of Andromeda. Which it failed to do.

But as Warren Cremer, a cultural anthropologist who ran a Jeep tour business, told me shortly afterward, "That was the exception. The movement has a clean intent. I don't see cranks or cults; I see people who are no longer satisfied with establishment medicine, science, or religion, and are looking for something else. They don't know how to go about it, exactly, but they're definitely non-confrontational, non-protestational. They're looking for a better planet and a better way of life, and in that, I support the community 100 percent."

Cremer's moderate line wasn't taken by all. Some who came after the Harmonic Convergence claimed to have experiences that can only be filed under woo-woo.

In a book titled *Sedona Starseed*, author Raymond Mardyks claimed, "There exists deep within Boynton Canyon an area used as a teleportation instrument . . . the Beings who travel (these) holes in space are from a planet that orbits an invisible star near Sirius."

In *Sedona: Psychic Energy Vortexes*, Dick Sutphen reported that a visitor laid some crystals beside a dry creek bed and watched a giant Indian woman rise from the canyon floor: "She stood about 200 feet tall and was dressed in white buckskin . . . she was beautiful."

New Agers also began building medicine wheels — circles of rocks five to 200 feet in diameter — on Coconino National Forest land around Sedona. Disciples called them a "reawakening of Native American wisdom." The Forest Service called them pollution.

"Disturbing any kind of natural feature," Ranger Bob Gillies told *Newsweek* in 1991, "is a selfish thing to do — like carving your initials in a tree."

The medicine wheels, the shops selling crystals and pyramids, and the practitioners of "shamanic healing" and "UFO contacts" attracted some hostility.

"These days, the woods (around Sedona) are chock-full of chanters, crystal therapists and prayer-wheel builders," growled William Porter in the *Arizona Republic* newspaper. "In other words, it's prime territory to reintroduce grizzly bears."

Pete A. Sanders Jr., who conducts spiritual workshops in Sedona, told me that his wife, a gifted-education teacher, has been told, "If you

Bell Rock: $150 for a seat
and still it failed to depart for
Andromeda. George Stocking

teach my child anything that's New Age, I'm taking him out of your program."

In a long afternoon's conversation, Sanders proved to be a reasonable spokesman for the vortex phenomenon, as convincing as anyone could be across the table from a professional skeptic. Sanders said he has a degree in biomedical chemistry from the Massachusetts Institute of Technology and skipped out on Harvard Medical School to pursue unconventional research into human mental, physical, and spiritual potential. This brought him to Sedona.

Sanders said the geographical vortexes around Sedona come in two forms: upflow, where energy bursts out of the earth; and inflow, where energy goes in. Sometimes these are cataloged as male and female vortexes. Upflow/male vortexes are mountain or mesa tops; inflow/female vortexes are associated with depressions and canyons. Male vortexes are energizing; females encourage introspection.

New Agers consider Cathedral Rock to be a feminine vortex. Larry Lindahl.

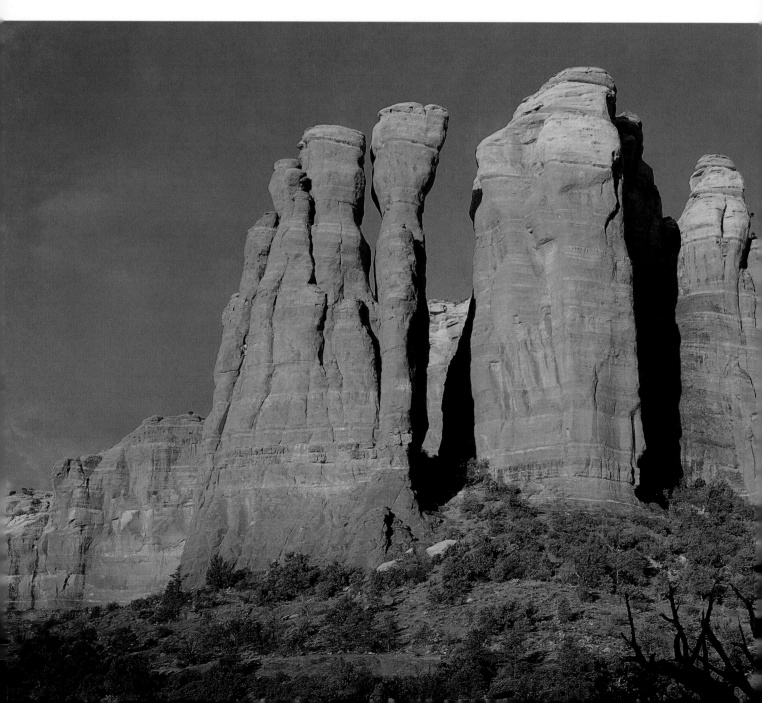

"If you go to these sites," Sanders said, "you literally see people walking differently. At some, they're chin down and reflective. At others, tall and confident. I'm hypothesizing that the same way there are currents in oceans and in the atmosphere, there are extradimensional currents in these sites that orient people's perceptions, and that we can 'ride' these currents in the same way that hawks and eagles ride thermals."

Both kinds of vortexes are valuable, he said. People come to Sedona trying to work things out, seeking inspiration "to be the best we can be, whether that comes through faith in God or faith in perseverance." The energy flow helps get us out of "our little bitty selves."

Despite his background in science, Sanders couldn't call his metaphorical hawks and eagles to earth. He doesn't know what kind of energy keeps them soaring or searching. He can't say whether belief in it is a matter of science, philosophy, or religion.

"It shouldn't be an either/or," he said. "Science is not the end-all of what is. It's just what we know so far."

I remain a vortex agnostic. I have been to all of the sites and have had no spiritual epiphanies, no tinglings of insight or energy. But I did once find myself on a Jeep tour of vortex sites with a clinical psychologist, a smart woman who was not predisposed to believe, either.

At the last stop, our guide nodded to one side, and said, "The energy comes from over there."

"No," the psychologist said, looking in a different direction. "It's coming from over there."

When You Go

All the Sedona vortexes, or power points, are easy to find. They tend to be busy. If lonely meditation is what you're seeking, go at dawn.

Bell Rock is the bell-shaped monolith off State Route 179 5.5 miles south of its "Y" junction with State Route 89A. There is no official trail and no agreed-upon point to experience the vortex power. Hikers and energy seekers have marked numerous routes to the upper mezzanines. The summit is difficult and intimidating; only spiders and rock climbers go there. This is said to be a masculine vortex.

Cathedral Rock is a feminine vortex, a ridge stretched between two peaks that offers awesome views. For directions, see Page 52.

Airport Mesa demands little or no hiking. Drive 1.1 miles on State 89A west of the "Y" junction and turn south on Airport Road. Some sources recommend parking at the dirt pullout half a mile up the mesa and walking east up the short trail. Others suggest driving all the way to the top and following the signs to the "Sunrise Service" and the Masonic Lodge Memorial Cross. This is a masculine vortex.

Boynton Canyon exudes both masculine and feminine energy, believers say. For directions, see Page 52. Some people climb up to formations in the canyon walls that seem to have energy or personal meaning to them. One hoodoo, or strangely shaped formation, on the east wall offers a womb-like space.

CHAPTER THREE

Outside Sedona

Amid Arizona's Finest

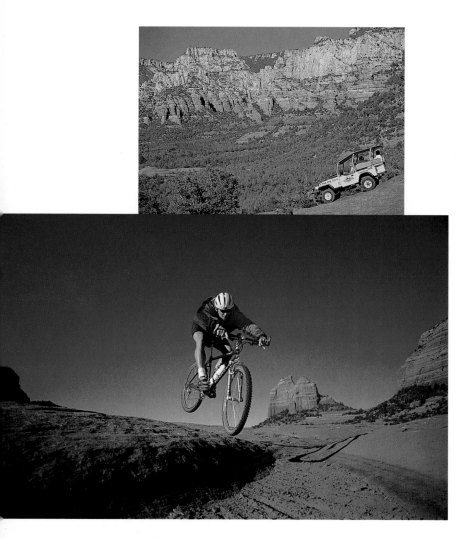

Sedona's climate and terrain invite people to get active.
Top: Jeeps take visitors right into the heart of red rock country, with Munds Mountain in the background. Tom Bean
Above: This bike rider extracts excitement from the red rocks in the Cow Pies area. Mike Padian
Right: The reward for pedaling up Schnebly Hill Road can be solitude and a fantastic view. Mike Padian

*I am alarmed when it happens
that I have walked a mile
into the woods bodily, without
getting there in spirit . . .
what business have I in the
woods, if I am thinking
of something out of the woods?*
— HENRY DAVID THOREAU
from his essay, Walking

Great, fat drops begin to splatter the windshield 30 seconds after I've paid my five bucks and passed a NO RAIN CHECKS sign at the entrance to Slide Rock State Park. I expected it — a sky the color of a stealth bomber's belly usually will do something like this.

But the rain doesn't ruin the day, not here. I wrap myself in a rain jacket and Seattle sombrero and leave the car for a day of hiking in Oak Creek Canyon and its tributaries. I stare at the towering west wall of the canyon, and even in the softness of the rain, the red and charcoal palisade assumes the craggy, Olympian mood of a late Beethoven sonata. Its power and mystery seem palpable. Low clouds probe into side canyons like ghosts slinking through dark alleys. Rain, splashing onto the sandstone sluice framing Oak Creek, paints it the color of a

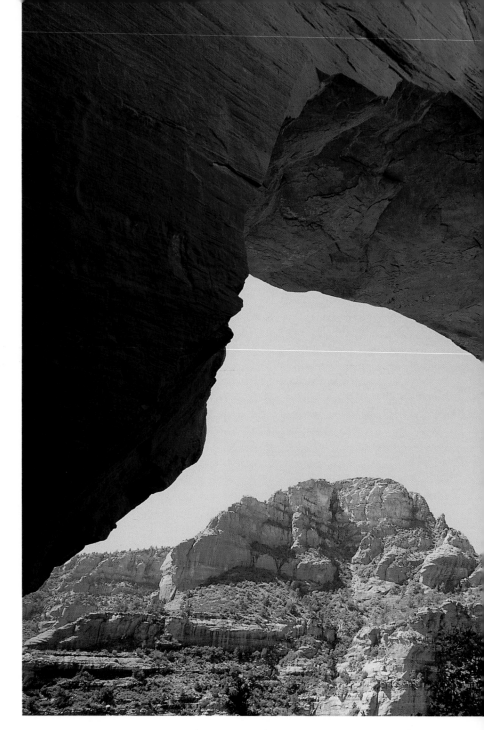

glistening king salmon fillet. Its improbable brilliance recalls the story about a Wisconsin pressman who, decades ago, throttled back the color on an *Arizona Highways* press run because he refused to believe rocks existed in such outrageous shades of red.

No rain check — who needs one? I'd pay double to be out here in this weather. The crowds evaporate. The creek begins to thrash more urgently. The natural drama of the canyon is enhanced. There is more than ever to see, a constellation of fresh extravaganza in the landscape. Thoreau, were he around, would find his thoughts fully engaged in the landscape at hand because it is so lovely and dramatic. I rarely daydream in the woods around Sedona. There's just not enough leftover brain capacity for it.

This is the best place to be outdoors in Arizona. The climate is amenable to all-season hiking, with a range of elevation from 4,300 feet around Sedona to 7,122 feet atop Wilson Mountain. The variety of scenery is astonishing and the supply of surprises unending. An unheralded Sinagua pueblo suddenly pops into view on the Lost Canyon Trail. A bizarre copse of oak trees, their trunks curling in unison to the south, greets me at Sterling Pass. There are wonderful sights to be bagged with hardly any exertion. Seven Sacred Pools, a queue of rain-collecting dimples on a sandstone ledge, is a half-mile stroll from the end of Soldier Pass Road.

And then there are routes that feel, with a full pack, more like death marches than hikes.

This land can also be hazardous, another characteristic that recommends Thoreauvian attention to the matters at hand. Rattlesnakes, for one. No need to fear, just be aware — and learn from the occasional encounters. I once met a diamondback on a trail in Sycamore Canyon 20 miles south of Sedona. We made eye contact from a respectful distance and engaged in a wordless negotiation: I agreed to circle 10 feet out of my way and not disturb his sunbath, and he agreed to not terminate my existence. I reflected on this during my next hour in the canyon. Negotiations with Nature are always clear and unambiguous. She never lies, never complains, never explains.

This 90-foot-long natural bridge is Fay Arch, one of the landmarks in the Red Rock-Secret Mountain Wilderness.
Bob & Suzanne Clemenz

the right words. ". . . Well, you just shouldn't do that."

There are several other guidelines for any form of outdoor recreation in the Sedona area. In addition to the standard caveats that apply to hiking and camping anywhere, remember these:

• Always carry more water than you think you'll need. The dry air, mountain topography, and steep rise in daytime temperature can cause dehydration sooner than you might expect. The standard formula for desert or arid mountain hiking applies everywhere around Sedona: one gallon per person per day.

• High elevation and bright sunlight mean a high risk of sunburn and, more ominously, melanoma. Wear a hat and use sunblock. Yes, in winter, too.

• That same high elevation and clear atmosphere translates into a serious risk of hypothermia if you're surprised by a storm or lost after dark. Temperatures plunge. Carry extra clothing, emergency food, a flashlight, and waterproof matches.

• Wear hiking boots. Most of the trails around the red rocks involve some steep ascending or slickrock scrambling where good traction is vital to your health. And don't commit fully to a foothold or handhold until you're certain you can trust it. Sandstone can crumble like a stale scone.

We invite trouble only when we show up without adequate respect.

Years ago, when I began hiking in the Sedona area, I lurched to the summit of Wilson Mountain. Alone and exhausted, I took out a Forest Service leaflet and read that the mountain was named for Richard Wilson, who had been grim-reaped right here in 1885, by a bear. I quietly slinked 3,000 feet back down to civilization and called Bob Gillies, then the ranger in charge of the Forest Service office in Sedona. He said he had not heard of any bear incidents in modern history. Sure, there are bears, he's seen them, but they stay away from people. Except: "If you have one cornered . . . " he began, then paused, hunting for

Route 89A between mileposts 376 and 377) and at Slide Rock State Park.

• Fishing is allowed anywhere on public property bordering Oak Creek with a state license. Arizona Game and Fish stocks it with non-native rainbow trout all year, most frequently in summer.

• Jeep tours have long been a popular and painless way to visit the backcountry around Sedona; several local operators offer them. Specialized tours may focus on archaeological sites, vortexes, or photographic opportunities. Reservations are advised.

• Aircraft tours provide another perspective. At this writing, adventurers can choose from hot-air balloons, helicopters, and open-cockpit biplanes.

Left: Trout lurk in the rocky underside of Oak Creek. Below: A Jeep scrambles just off Schnebly Hill Road. Both by Bob & Suzanne Clemenz Right: Fat-tired bikes were made for terrain like this area called Cow Pies. Mike Padian

• Many Coconino National Forest trails in the area are multi-use, so follow this trail etiquette: Mountain bikes yield to hikers and horses; hikers yield to horses.

The range of outdoor sports and other pursuits around Sedona is limited only by the imagination and instinct for self-preservation. Whatever your inclination, this is no place to stay indoors, whatever the weather. Here are some possibilities:

Rainbow Trout And Lifetime Vows

Since Sedona's tourism boom began, people have been discovering and inventing opportunities to experience the landscape. Some of this you can do on your own; in other cases, local for-profit enterprises are set up to guide you.

• Swimming is possible in tiny Oak Creek, most rewardingly at Grasshopper Point swim area (just off State

• Weddings among the red rocks are a booming cottage industry. Several local planners arrange settings, music, photography, catering, and honeymoons.

Golf

Three courses are open to the public: Poco Diablo Resort has a nine-hole course and both Sedona Golf Resort and Oak Creek Country Club have 18 holes. Scenery is a hazard to concentration.

Mountain Biking

A decade ago, mountain biking around Sedona was nearly as rare as kayaking; now it's exploding in popularity. Great bike trails have been around for generations, but only recently have mountain bikes truly welcomed riders to those trails. The critical development: double suspension.

"Sedona's a rough spot," local bike shop owner Rama Jon says, "but the body doesn't have to take all that pain anymore. Now the suspension takes it." He adds that the average age of resident mountain bikers in Sedona is probably 10 years older than anywhere else in the Southwest. One local club calls itself "The Gnarly Old Dudes."

Most of the high desert hiking trails around the red rocks double as mountain bike trails. Jeep roads lace the area, and all of these are great for biking. Oak Creek Canyon trails

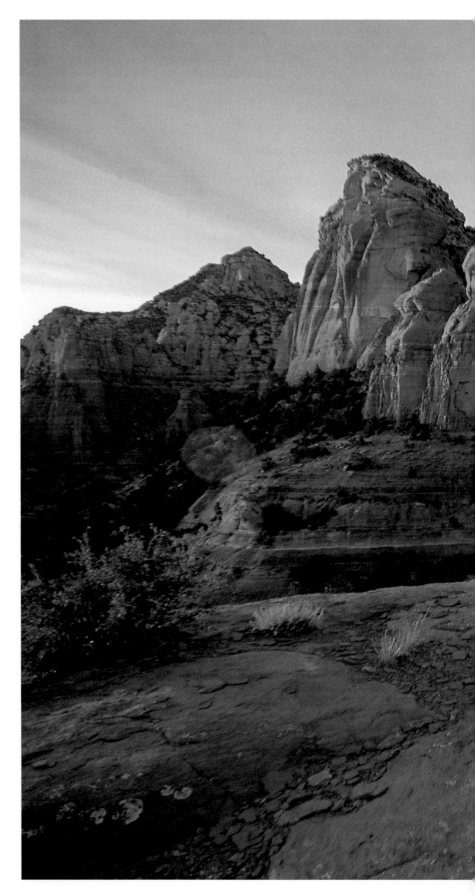

These campers have set up on Steamboat Rock in the Red Rock-Secret Mountain Wilderness. Tom Bean

generally are too steep, and mountain bikes are not allowed in designated wilderness.

Rock Climbing

Why go climbing in the red rocks?

"Because they're close," said Dave Keeber, Sedona Library director and climbing enthusiast. "And because rock climbers are nuts."

Seriously, although rock climbing is growing in popularity here, Sedona is no place for the inexpert climber. The formations are tantalizing, but the material is treacherous. The Kaibab (red) and Coconino (tan) sandstone of the red rocks is very soft and crumbly.

Keeber recommends one basalt cliff, which is much more stable: directly under Oak Creek Vista where State Route 89A climbs out of Oak Creek Canyon.

Camping

In 1995, the Forest Service estimated that 200,000 people camped out in the woods, mountains, and canyons around Sedona. That number rang alarm bells in the Forest Service's rustic office on Brewer Road, because it is more than officials believe the environment can tolerate. A new forest management plan is in the works, and it will mean more restrictions for campers.

"We recognize that camping has important value," District Ranger Ken Anderson explained. "But there are very limited resources here. You're going to have to plan ahead if you want to camp."

The Forest Service operates overnight campgrounds with a total of just 178 spaces in the area. Backpack camping is allowed in the Coconino National Forest except where there are special rules, such as the first six miles of the West Fork of Oak Creek.

The Forest Service also maintains a limited number of campsites for RVs and/or trailers in Oak Creek Canyon. Call well in advance to reserve space. There is a seven-day stay limit on all campgrounds. There are also several commercial RV campsites in the Sedona area.

Forest Service campgrounds from Sedona north on State Route 89A into Oak Creek Canyon are:

MANZANITA (between mileposts 380 and 381). Water, toilets; RVs but no trailers. Open year round. 19 sites.

BANJO BILL (between mileposts 382 and 383). Water, toilets; RVs but no trailers. Open March through October. Eight sites.

BOOTLEGGER (at Milepost 383). Toilets; RVs but no trailers. Open March through October. 10 sites.

CAVE SPRINGS (between mileposts 385 and 386). Water, toilets; RVs and trailers to 36 feet. Open April 26 through September. 80 sites.

PINEFLAT EAST/PINEFLAT WEST (between mileposts 386 and 387). Water, toilets; RVs and trailers to 36 feet. Open March until first heavy snow. 58 sites, including two handicap accessible.

Hiking

Sedona is surrounded by government-designated wilderness areas — the Red Rock-Secret Mountain Wilderness to the north and the Munds Mountain Wilderness to the south, both pieces of the Coconino National Forest. Between them, and on adjoining state lands, are more than 100 hikes. Some are well-maintained and signed Forest Service trails, some are old Jeep or horse trails, and still others are informal routes cataloged by assorted private guidebooks. All these vary greatly in accessibility and difficulty, but they have one thing in common: None is dull.

Because hiking in the area is so popular, the Forest Service has embarked on an ambitious program to expand the trail system, improve the signage, and protect the environment by limiting group size and emphasizing environmental etiquette. An increasing problem is "user-created" trails, which mislead hikers and trample undergrowth needlessly. Although the Forest Service has not yet prohibited off-trail hiking, rangers are working to discourage it — with good reason.

Consider the season when planning a hike. Shady forest trails above 6,000 feet may be blocked by snow or ice in winter. Exposed routes are less enchanting in summer, although half-day hikes from dawn to late morning are cool enough in Sedona, even in July. If you crave solitude, stay away from Boynton Canyon and the West Fork of Oak Creek during peak tourist times. In fact, saving these trails for a rainy day is the

Cathedral Rock Trail climbs 760 feet in less than a mile. David H. Smith

only way of avoiding the crowds.

Here are 10 glorious and greatly varied day hikes in the Sedona area. The first seven weave around and upon the red rocks, and the last three start in Oak Creek Canyon. Mileages are one way, and difficulty ratings assume an experienced, middle-age hiker of average ability and determination — me.

LITTLE HORSE TRAIL (one mile, easy) is a little difficult to follow because of the many false trails meandering off from it, but it's impossible to get lost — just keep Twin Buttes in sight, which is easy to do since the trail skirts their south base. Snuggling up so close to these monoliths is a remarkable introduction to the power of the red rocks, and it's entirely different from the view through a windshield. Look for the unmarked trailhead about halfway up the driveway to the Chapel of the Holy Cross; it's on the east side.

CATHEDRAL ROCK TRAIL (0.7 mile, moderate) is short but very steep, climbing 760 feet in less than a mile. The Forest Service has marked it with permanent wire-basket cairns and has chiseled helpful footholds in the sandstone. Trail's end is a crescent-shaped saddle between the sheer vertical towers of the "cathedral," with great views of the riparian scribble of Oak Creek. This is a feminine vortex, said to be good for unwinding from a high-stress job. Go 3.4 miles south on State Route 179 from the Sedona "Y", turn right on "Back-o-Beyond," and drive 0.7 mile to trailhead parking.

BELL ROCK TRAIL (three miles, easy) is for the most part a Jeep road that circumnavigates the bell-shaped landmark south of Sedona. Vortex seekers scramble up the sandstone ledges to the rock's higher elevations, although there is no clearly defined trail. Go south 5.6 miles from the "Y" on State Route 179; park at Milepost 308.

BOYNTON CANYON (three miles, easy) is, with good reason, the Sedona area's most popular hike; the red canyon walls contain and define a miniature world of drop-dead geological and botanical beauty. You'll hike through a forest of manzanita and visit (in season) the rapids of a foot-wide creek. There are perhaps 50 Sinagua ruins in this canyon, all so well concealed by their prehistoric architects you'll probably never see them. The Forest Service is considering banning hiking to the ruins because of Native American concerns. Take Dry Creek Road 2.9 miles north from State Route 89A in west Sedona, turn left on Boynton Pass Road, and drive 1.6 miles to trailhead parking.

FAY CANYON (1.1 miles, easy to moderate) offers the option of a scramble up a steep, unmaintained trail for a firsthand encounter with a natural arch. Take the fork to the right at the half-mile mark if you're up for the adventure; otherwise you won't see the arch from the main trail. Take Dry Creek Road 2.9 miles north from State Route 89A in west Sedona. Turn left on Boynton Pass Road. Look for trailhead parking on the right a half mile after the road turns to gravel.

Hikers climb a trail above Wet Beaver Creek. Tom Bean

LOST CANYON (2.2 miles, moderate) has an appropriate name — not many hikers have found it (yet), so you can expect solitude. Unlike most of the area's canyon hikes, this trail follows a ledge rather than the canyon floor. Acrophobics may find it unsettling. Sinagua ruins are visible along the trail. Take Dry Creek Road two miles north from State Route 89A in west Sedona. Turn right on Forest Service Road 152 and follow it 2.5 miles to the trailhead. Begin on the Brins Mesa Trail, follow it for 200 feet, then take the trail to the right.

SEVEN SACRED POOLS (0.5 mile, easy) is an unofficial hike — really, just a stroll — to a string of rain-collecting natural depressions in a cascade of sandstone ledges. It's definitely worth investigation if there's been rain in the last few days. Take Soldier Pass Road 1.5 miles north from State Route 89A in west Sedona, turn right, and park at the end of the last

subdivision. Hike north 0.5 mile on dirt road, then look for ribbons in trees to the right indicating path to the pools.

STERLING PASS (2.4 miles, strenuous) also corkscrews 1,120 feet up the west wall of Oak Creek Canyon to a weird copse of oak trees, all straining southward to grasp the spare light. Although the trail is heavily wooded, there are several spectacular views into the canyons below along the way. Take State Route 89A into Oak Creek Canyon. The trailhead is 0.6 mile north of Milepost 380. There is little dedicated parking; do your best.

A.B. YOUNG TRAIL (1.6 miles, strenuous) once was a cattle trail, which may make you wonder whether Oak Creek Canyon ranchers were conditioning their cows for marathons. This trail ascends 1,700 feet through three distinct botanical zones — riparian, high desert, and conifer — in a scant mile and a half. At the top, you

may continue another 1.25 miles (and 400 feet of elevation gain) to a fire lookout tower at 7,196 feet. Take State Route 89A into Oak Creek Canyon. The trailhead is just north of Milepost 383.

WEST FORK OF OAK CREEK (three miles, moderate) should be renamed "The Canyon the Moon Cannot Find," the irresistible and evocative title given it by the late *Arizona Highways* writer William E. Hafford. This is one of Arizona's great hikes, a cool, shadowy canyon where concave walls leap over the creek like ocean waves frozen for eternity. The first three miles are relatively flat and easy, although wading is seasonally necessary. Experienced backpackers can continue, with some difficulty, for nine more miles. Take State Route 89A 10 miles north of Sedona. Parking (there's a charge) is just north of Milepost 384.

Finally, for visitors who want a sampler of red rock hiking

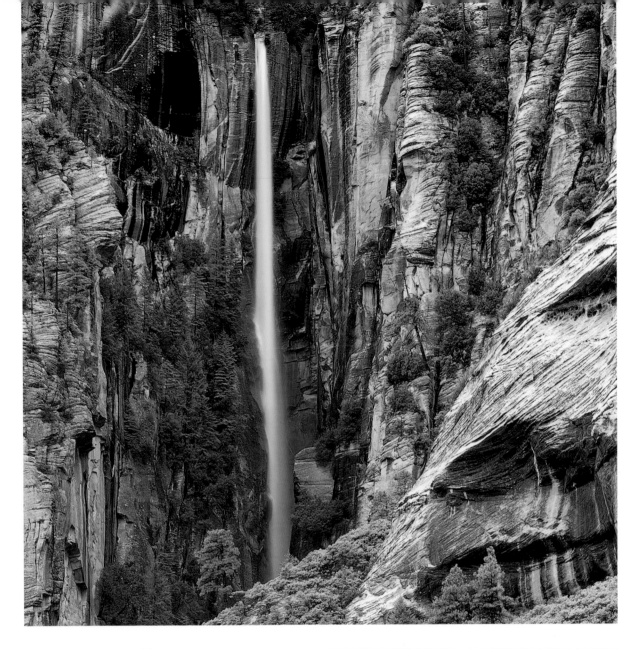

without the word "wilderness" hanging around, Red Rock State Park offers nine easy and wonderfully scenic trails ranging from 0.4 to 1.9 miles in length. One is wheelchair accessible. Ranger-guided moonlight walks are given monthly under the full moon, April through October.

Left: The going's relatively easy for the first three miles of the trail along the West Fork of Oak Creek. Then, as this hiker sees, the canyon narrows and hiking turns to rock scrambling. Tom Bean
Above: Rain produces ephemeral waterfalls in Oak Creek Canyon. Robert G. McDonald

When You Go

For further hiking and camping information, contact Coconino National Forest, Sedona Ranger District, P.O. Box 300, Sedona, AZ 86339. (520) 282-4119.

Red Rock State Park is at 4050 Red Rock Loop Road, Sedona, AZ 86336. (520) 282-6907.

Slide Rock State Park is just north of Milepost 381 on State Route 89A in Oak Creek Canyon. (520) 282-3034.

For mountain biking information, visit Mountain Bike Heaven's Web site at www.mountainbikeheaven.com/

For information on golf, Jeep tours, balloon flights, private campgrounds, and all other commercial outdoor activities, contact the Sedona-Oak Creek Canyon Chamber of Commerce, P.O. Box 478, Sedona, AZ 86339. (520) 282-7722.

Photographing Sedona:
THE PROMISED LAND

To a photographer arriving from almost anywhere else, Arizona looks like the promised land. The bravura landforms, the drama of fierce light and cryptic shadow, the choreography of gunmetal thunderclouds rumbling over a mountain or canyon offer endless opportunities — and challenges. Photographing Arizona can be a life's work.

In fact, photographing a 20-mile radius around Sedona could be a life's work. The intrigue and beauty are extravagant, and the weather guarantees eternal variety. Sedona is not only a place artists move to; it's a place where people become artists.

Sedona doesn't ask for much specialized equipment, but one accessory is very helpful: a tripod. You'll be shooting low-light pictures at dawn or dusk, preferably with low-speed film. Two filters are good to have: an 81a, which helps reduce color film's tendency to go blue in deep shadow or dark overcast, and a polarizer, which will darken a sun-bleached sky and block the reflections off the red rocks, intensifying their color.

Sedona does ask for patience. As far as photography is concerned, the red rocks are at their worst in the conditions we humans like best: warm, dry air and clear, blue sky. Use this time for

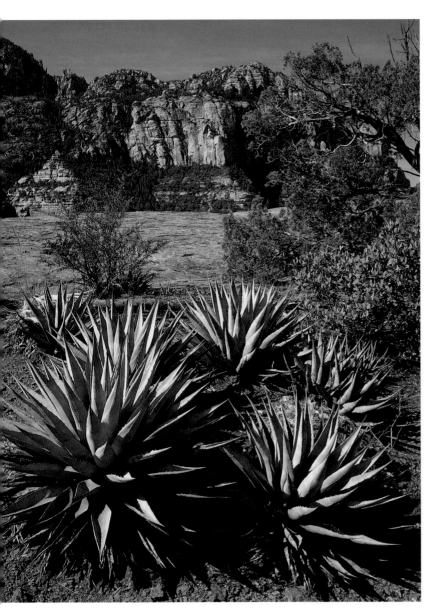

Far left: Autumn lays a colorful carpet over a wash in Oak Creek Canyon. Bob & Suzanne Clemenz
Left: A cluster of agaves stands out on a mesa alongside Schnebly Hill Road. Gary Ladd

So don't go there on a typical evening. Save such obvious shots for lousy weather, when everyone else will be indoors cursing the rain, and you'll have a chance of engaging the landscape in a different mood. Oak Creek Canyon's fall color party can be just another pretty photographic cliché, so search for the telling detail. A single golden sycamore leaf floating in a pool probably will tell a more powerful story than blotches of color on a distant mountainside.

When I photograph Sedona, I'm armed with ideas I've absorbed from working with dozens of photographers who spend a major part of their lives putting Arizona on film. Here are three excellent tips:

• The "180-degree rule" from Gary Ladd: When shooting landscapes in any dramatic lighting, turn around frequently to see what's happening behind you.

• The "near-far" technique of David Muench: Build a landscape from the nearest detail to the farthest horizon with every element in focus. This not only makes a sharp artistic statement, but an affirmation that all nature is a community, each piece equally vital to the integrity of the whole.

• "Creative patience" from Sedona's Bob Clemenz: "A lot of people get overwhelmed by the place and start shooting wildly. One of the things we do [in annual Sedona photographic workshops] is make four-by-five-inch cardboard 'picture finders.' Then we have the students put their cameras down. Somehow, they get a lot more creative with the finders. But probably the best advice for any photographer here is simply to stay around for a few days and begin to know the place."

Good advice, indeed. The only trouble is that it may turn a weekend affair into a lifetime obsession.

scouting locations and planning angles for sunset and sunrise shots. The rocks will appear the deepest red at sunset, because any dust in the air kicked up by the day's breeze will color the late light in the amber-orange-red end of the spectrum. But you won't have much time; sunsets in dry, clear air spoil quickly. I once measured the window of opportunity for an evening session with Cathedral Rock: seven minutes. Any shots earlier or later would have been wasting film.

Finding fresh images of Sedona may seem like a daunting challenge. Red Rock Crossing is sometimes said to be the most photographed scene in Arizona, which is easy to believe on a typical evening — a dozen photographers will be out there hopping rocks in the creek, jockeying for position.

CHAPTER FOUR

Day Trips

*Ventures to Oak Creek Canyon,
Ancient Sites, the Verde Valley, and Jerome*

The very forest-fringed earth seemed to have opened into a deep abyss, ribbed by red rock walls and choked by steep mats of green timber. The chasm was a V-shaped split and so deep that looking downward sent at once a chill and a shudder over Carley . . . What a wild, lonely, terrible place!

— ZANE GREY

from The Call of the Canyon *(1924)*

Night fell on a Sinagua Indian ruin under the brow of a red sandstone butte some 20 miles from midtown Sedona. In the last moments of light, the surrounding mountains seemed to turn violet, then smoky purple, then black against an indigo sky. There was a visitor here, a wilderness guide who went by the name of Ropes. He sensed that something was wrong.

"I'd been coming to this ruin in the daylight for 15 years," he said. "Once it got dark, it seemed so different. I got a real uneasy feeling — like I was intruding."

Ropes was no flake. He seemed to know as much about the ruin as an archaeologist. He knew that night, for example,

Residents of Verde Valley and nearby mountains have left different imprints of their culture. Top: The Sinagua people left stories with figures carved into rocks. Larry Lindahl Above: A mansion in Jerome built by copper-mining magnate James Douglas remains as Jerome State Historic Park and a symbol of the wealth extracted from the mountains. George H.H. Huey Right: Copper is a color in this legacy left by nature in Oak Creek Canyon. Bob & Suzanne Clemenz

that he was bunking down in what might have been a nursery. The winter sun would have angled in to make this the warmest room in the pueblo, and there were impressions of tiny fingerprints that had been pressed into the red clay mortar in the walls 800 years ago. He also suspected that beneath the bare earth floor were burial sites. A Sinagua custom was to bury children's bodies under the pueblo, possibly so their spirits would benefit from the proximity of living parents.

"I was on the verge of drifting off to sleep," Ropes told me. "And then I heard crying. At first, I tried to tell myself that it was bats. Then I thought, well, it's jackrabbits. Finally I realized I was hearing children. Crying, in this room. I kind of chilled out, let the hair come back down on my neck, tried to go to sleep again. And every time I was on the verge of sleep, I'd be awakened by these ungodly sounds. Children crying. It felt like tears in there. All night, it felt like tears."

Ropes' experience may have been unnatural, but it isn't unusual. Wherever Southwestern prehistory is exposed, as it is all around Sedona, you hear variations on it. People encounter crows or snakes around the ruins and have the disquieting feeling that they aren't ordinary animals, but sentinels. Or they find a "souvenir" artifact, take it home, and suffer an inexplicable string of illnesses and accidents. Several years ago, after I had collected a substantial file of these stories, I phoned three archaeologists for comment. I

expected them to scoff. They didn't. Two of the three described strange encounters they had had.

Of course, there are many attractions other than prehistoric pueblos in northern Arizona, and most of us have perfectly normal and pleasant experiences when we do visit the ruins — in the daylight. But the land itself is enchanted; it frequently works magic on our spirits and emotions.

"Certain places take us beyond ourselves," wrote Flagstaff author Scott Thybony in *Burntwater*, and such places seem to present themselves in whatever direction a traveler radiates from Sedona.

Most visitors never investigate the wealth of possibilities within a two- or three-hour drive, and their lives — I think — are poorer for the failure. I've been having breakfast with assorted strangers at a Sedona bed-and-breakfast, and someone will say, "We have a whole day. What should we see?" I stifle the urge to scold — a week should be mandatory — and fetch an Arizona map.

Oak Creek Canyon

Zane Grey's 1924 novel *The Call of the Canyon* could have profited if he had shed a few adjectives from the overheated prose, or so I thought before I talked with Bob Kittredge. Wild, lonely, terrible? Oak Creek Canyon had never seemed so to me, not with 2.9 million cars a year beetling along the 12 miles of State Route 89A on the canyon floor. But Kittredge had grown up in the canyon in the

1950s, in a log cabin by the creek, and his childhood memories reflected Grey's descriptions.

It was indeed lonely, he said. Civilization seemed as distant as another planet. His company was not the birds and chipmunks that charm tourists today, but an old radio he kept by the bed, pulling in clear channel KOMA from some place called Oklahoma City. A family excursion to Phoenix was a major production; the drive each way then took four or five hours.

There was one advantage, he said: "I learned very early to be resilient. I had to depend on myself for my entertainment."

But to a little kid, the canyon was overpowering. The scale of everything was too large. Once the sight of a bear cub, a plump fur ball hardly larger than a dog, scared him out of his wits. At

Oak Creek usually runs clear, cold, and shallow, coursing its way over rocks and under a canopy of tree limbs.
Dick Dietrich

65

night, the trees were shadowy
monsters with arms poised to
snatch him. Once he fell off a
horse while crossing Oak Creek,
and it seemed like a river 60 feet
wide.

He grew up and moved
away.

"I swore I would never come
back here," he told me. When he
tentatively returned many years
later, he felt claustrophobic.
There were no horizons, only
canyon walls squeezing away the
sky.

"I finally came to feel the
canyon as a place of refuge," he
said, "but it's been a long
process. And I find it interesting
that none of the kids who grew
up here at the time I did today
lives in the canyon — or, for that
matter, in any canyon."

Drive the highway, stop
briefly at the popular
attractions, and you are unlikely
to feel such complicated
sensations. But Oak Creek
Canyon is still an easy place to
get lost, figuratively, and when
you are alone with the canyon, it
can be a very powerful place.

The first English-speaking
human to stake a·claim to the
canyon was Jim Thompson, an
Irishman who ran away from
home in Londonderry at 11,
then kicked around the
Wild West as a pioneering
jack-of-all-trades. When he
found his way into Oak Creek
Canyon in 1876 at what is now
called Indian Gardens (Milepost
378), he found, literally, Indian
gardens of corn, squash, and
beans. The Tonto Apaches had
farmed the site not long before,
and some of their crops were
still popping up. Thompson built
a log cabin, began cultivating his

own crops, and eventually
brought his family.

A trickle of pioneers
followed. In 1907, Frank
Pendley homesteaded a sloping
meadow above Slide Rock,
trapped bobcats for bounty, and
planted fruit trees. His orchards,
now on state park land, still
produce apples. In 1930,
Kittredge's father, Bob Sr.,
bought property and a dream
and, 16 years later, moved out

With the San Francisco Peaks on the
horizon, Oak Creek Canyon unfolds
to the north from Mount Wilson.
Larry Lindahl

from New York because he
craved solitude. Soon a
sprinkling of rustic tourist cabins
appeared. By the 1950s, the fact
that Oak Creek Canyon had
that one vital amenity, a paved
road through it, guaranteed, for

better or worse, that it would become one of Arizona's most popular destinations.

The first thing you notice, funneling into the canyon from Sedona, are the tops of the canyon walls. They aren't planar ridgelines butting against the sky, but an arcade of fanciful sculptures: a mitten, a thumb, a potbellied gargoyle. Layers of sandstone and limestone, each of a different texture and strength, have eroded and crumbled into cartoons.

The creek itself is another lovely attraction, a cold, crystalline, all-season waterway in a state where nearly every other river runs unreliably or ruddy with sediment. Unless it's

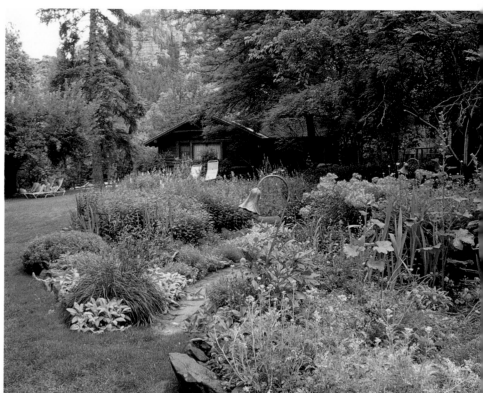

been raining heavily somewhere in its watershed, Oak Creek runs just two or three feet deep and 10 to 15 feet wide, gurgling a desultory course around smooth, black boulders, shaded by oak and sycamore trees that in many places form a full canopy across the water. Fish (and therefore fishermen) find it an amenable habitat — more than 20 species live in the creek, and the Arizona Game and Fish Department stocks it with non-native rainbow trout.

Slide Rock State Park, the old Pendley homestead, is the

Above: Garland's Oak Creek Lodge is tucked neatly alongside Oak Creek, providing civilized pleasures. Bob & Suzanne Clemenz
Left: Slide Rock State Park is a place where crowds frolic in the water and slide down a natural sandstone sluice. Dick Dietrich

most popular place in the canyon to get acquainted with the creek, although I can't recommend it in midsummer. A typical July day brings 1,600 strollers and swimmers, and particularly on weekends, it seems more like a Southern California beach party than any sylvan communion.

The "slide" down a natural sandstone sluice in the creek is great family fun but not without natural risk.

"We have injuries all the time," a park ranger said.

There's more sedate creek swimming at Grasshopper Point (between mileposts 376 and 377), just north of uptown Sedona.

There are also civilized pleasures in the canyon. One of Arizona's best dining

Clumps of sedges and smooth, black rocks form a striking scene in Oak Creek. Larry Ulrich

experiences is tucked improbably into the forest halfway up the canyon. It's difficult to get a bunk for the night at Garland's Oak Creek Lodge — the regulars book their cabins a year in advance and cancel only under dire circumstances — but dinner reservations are relatively easy to get.

The lodge has been around in some form since the mid-1930s and in the Garland family since 1972, so its traditions may be rooted more deeply than any other commercial enterprise in the Sedona area. Arriving for dinner one evening, I stared at the heroic blaze in the lodge's massive fireplace and felt an echo of that sensation William O. Douglas described: being part of something much bigger than myself, "something great and majestic and wholesome."

Dinner that night was at least great and wholesome:

When You Go

Oak Creek Canyon Spring and fall are Oak Creek Canyon's best seasons. Summer finds it packed, and some of the cabins close in winter. Some hiking trails are likely to be blocked by snow or ice. Fall color usually peaks around mid-October, although this varies with the elevation.

Slide Rock State Park is open year round. (520) 282-3034. Grasshopper Point, a national forest picnic and swimming area, closes November through February. Other national forest picnic areas are open year-round. For campground information, see Page 50.

Roadside parking in the canyon is limited. Pullouts near the popular hiking trailheads are small and fill up early in the day. Avoid blocking private driveways. There is pay parking at the West Fork of Oak Creek.

Garland's Oak Creek Lodge is open April through mid-November. (520) 282-3343.

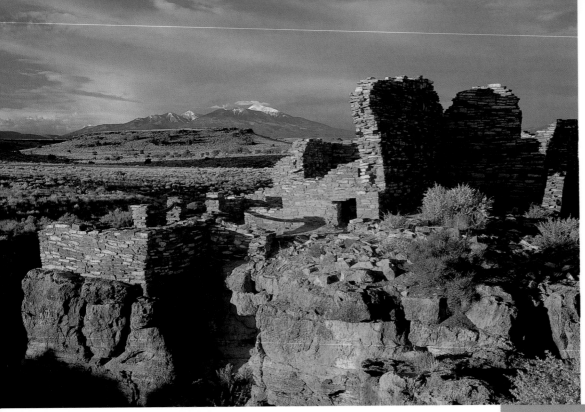

Left: Lomaki is one of the ruins at Wupatki National Monument, 60 miles northeast of Sedona. Tom Danielsen
Below: These Sinaguan ruins are preserved at Tuzigoot National Monument. Dick Dietrich

tortilla soup sparkling with the flavors of lime and green Anaheim chiles; a salad of red leaf lettuce, jicama, and pomegranate seeds bathed in orange sesame vinaigrette; and a perfect filet mignon lathered with a tart tomatillo sauce. You don't order at Garland's. The kitchen serves whatever they've dreamed up, picked from the garden, or caught. It isn't nouvelle, but it sure isn't cowboy cooking, either. Nor do you pick your dinner companions. You're as likely to be seated at a table with Diane Sawyer (as my tablemates said they were last time) as with . . . me.

Upstream from Garland's, the highway continues to hug the creek for another half-dozen miles, and then it corkscrews out of the canyon onto the Colorado Plateau for the short run through alpine forest to Flagstaff. There's a last stop at the rim, Oak Creek Vista, that offers a spectacular view into the canyon. This, or some place close to it, must have been where Carley Burke, Zane Grey's female lead in *The Call of the Canyon*, first stared into the abyss:

"Carley had never gazed upon a scene like this. Hostile and prejudiced, she yet felt wrung from her an acknowledgment of beauty and grandeur. But wild, violent, savage! Not livable. This insulated rift in the crust of the earth was a gigantic burrow for beasts, perhaps for outlawed men — not for a civilized person."

Carley, of course, lived there happily ever after. And civilization came to the canyon — but not so much so that the wildness entirely vanished.

The Sinagua World

Can a prehistoric experience change a contemporary life? Half an hour at a prehistoric ruin named Honanki, a Hopi word meaning "Bear House", did so for me. I was on an "ancient ruins" Jeep tour out of Sedona with three other visitors

and a well-qualified and provocative guide who taught Southwestern prehistory at the college level. When we stopped at Honanki, I first felt a twinge of disappointment. Only a fraction of what had once been an impressive 60-room pueblo remained. But the story line was seductive. Honanki was built around A.D. 1150 and abandoned a little more than a century later, like most of the ruined pueblos around Sedona. Why? Our guide ticked off the standard possibilities: drought, warfare, soil exhaustion. None adequately explained it. He then led us to a petroglyph, a picture etched in the red sandstone cliff overhanging Honanki, and suggested a radical interpretation: It was a comet, which had served as a cosmic sign to begin a great migration.

I was dubious, and I remain so today. But that moment ignited my curiosity. Over the next six years, I prowled every publicly accessible prehistoric ruin in the Southwest, interviewed scores of archaeologists, and finally wrote an *Arizona Highways* book (*A.D. 1250: Ancient Peoples of the Southwest*) to try to illuminate that shadowy question: What happened to them?

Hundreds of these prehistoric pueblos huddle in the red canyons around Sedona. Hundreds more are strewn across the Verde Valley, to the south, and there are literally thousands on the Colorado Plateau to the north. Those closest to Sedona were built by the Sinagua people, who confound modern archaeologists. "Sinagua," a Spanish compound word that means "without water," describes only their environment — average annual rainfall at their pueblo sites today ranges

from seven to 20 inches. But there were too many variations in their art, architecture, and burial practices for archaeologists to classify them as a single, coherent culture.

They may have been a composite of others, or they might have been a medley of people not even unified by a common language.

You meet the Sinagua identity crisis head-on at Wupatki National Monument, 60 miles northeast of Sedona. This chilly, austere desert in the rain shadow of the San Francisco Peaks seems an unlikely harbor for any civilization, let alone one that didn't have the technology to move water and food over long distances. But there are about 2,000 Sinagua ruins sprinkled around Wupatki, and it appears to have been an important prehistoric crossroads.

The national monument shows off the Sinagua culture at its most ambitious with Wupatki Pueblo, a 100-room apartment building behind the visitors center. But is it really Sinaguan? To anyone versed in prehistoric Southwestern architecture, its form looks strikingly like the "great houses" of New Mexico's

Chaco Canyon, which began to be abandoned around A.D. 1130 — very close to the time that Wupatki was built. Its masonry looks like Kayenta Anasazi, and the abandonment of Wupatki began around 1225, just as the Kayenta building boom began at Navajo National Monument,

Left: A warm spring feeds Montezuma Well, a part of Montezuma Castle National Monument. George H.H. Huey Below: Visitors can walk by this reconstructed dwelling at Walnut Canyon National Monument. Laurence Parent

100 miles farther northeast. Wupatki Pueblo also includes a sunken ball court, which suggests that its inhabitants, whoever they were, had plugged into the ceremonial sports conference of the desert Hohokam people around present-day Phoenix. "Whoever they were..." sounds like an eternal qualifier for the people of Wupatki.

But their architecture was,

and is, breathtaking. Every time I visit Sedona, I schedule one morning's departure for 4 or 5 o'clock, depending on the season, so I can arrive at Wupatki's Wukoki Ruin for sunrise. This little building, which probably sheltered an extended Sinagua family, buds from a sandstone outcropping with such organic grace that it is

Wukoki probably housed an extended Sinaguan family.
Laurence Parent

as if God had turned to the human masons and said, "I'm tired of working on this rock; you finish the job." At sunrise or sunset, the red desert is bathed in fire colors, there is never anyone else around, and I am wrapped in the counterpoint of profound beauty and immense loneliness. It is tempting to imagine that the Sinaguans felt this way 800 years ago.

Outside the rain shadow, 30 miles to the south, the Sinagua also occupied Walnut Canyon, a forested 385-foot-deep furrow in

the ponderosa forest. Though not as dramatic as the Wupatki ruins, some of the 300 dwellings in Walnut Canyon National Monument have been stabilized and repaired. Visitors can peer inside for a valuable demonstration of how confining, cold, and dark Sinagua apartments actually were.

The southern branch of the Sinagua is preserved at two more national monuments in the Verde Valley: Montezuma Castle and Tuzigoot.

Sinagua people tucked this three-story dwelling — misleadingly named Montezuma Castle — into an alcove in a limestone cliff. George H.H. Huey

When You Go

The Sinagua World   It isn't possible to design a single day trip to explore the Sinagua world — it's too big. Split it into northern and southern Sinagua — which more and more archaeologists are inclined to do.

Northern Sinagua: You might not think you want to do this, but consider leaving Sedona at 4 or 5 A.M. for the two-hour drive into Wupatki National Monument. The park is open at all hours, and the turnoff to Wukoki Ruin is easy to find, even in the first strain of morning light. It's the paved spur to the right 23 miles from the south park entrance. The 46-mile-long loop road also passes four other ruins and Sunset Crater, a volcano that last erupted in A.D. 1064-65. (520) 679-2365.

Return to U.S. Route 89 after the morning in Wupatki, head south for Flagstaff, and turn east on Interstate 40 to Walnut Canyon National Monument. The three-quarter-mile trail to the ruins descends and climbs 185 feet and is worth the moderate effort. (520) 526-3367.

For the afternoon, visit the Museum of Northern Arizona three miles northwest of Flagstaff on Fort Valley Road (U.S. Route 180). This superb museum, founded in 1928, has a vast territory to cover — the sciences and cultures of the entire Colorado Plateau — but the permanent exhibit on the native peoples of the region, including the Sinagua, is thorough and fascinating. (520) 774-5213.

Southern Sinagua: Palatki and Honanki, two small ruins near Sedona, are administered by the National Forest Service. Take State Route 89A west 9.5 miles from the "Y" intersection with State Route 179 in Sedona. Turn right on Forest Service Road 525, drive six miles to where FR 795 branches to the right, and take FR 795 two miles to its dead end. The trail to the north leads 0.2 mile to Palatki, and the trail to the west leads 0.2 mile to a petroglyph site. For Honanki, continue on FR 525 another 3.2 miles beyond its intersection with FR 795. For more information, call Coconino National Forest Sedona Ranger District, (520) 282-4119.

After Palatki and Honanki, return to State Route 89A and continue south to Tuzigoot National Monument, (520) 634-5564), and Montezuma Castle National Monument, (520) 567-5276.

Archaeological Etiquette and Felonies   The Arizona Antiquities Act of 1960 made it a felony to remove or damage prehistoric artifacts from state-owned land. The U.S. Archaeological Resources Protection Act of 1979 protects artifacts on federal land. A prehistoric potsherd stashed in someone's desk drawer is meaningless; that same fragment left in the context where it fell a millennium past might someday help archaeologists fill in some blanks in our understanding of the ancient peoples of the Southwest. Take only photographs; leave only footprints.

Montezuma Castle was badly misnamed by U.S. Army scouts who stumbled across it in the 1860s. It was built at least two centuries before the reign of the final Aztec emperor, who never came within a thousand miles of Arizona. But it is a remarkably ambitious structure, some 65 rooms filling a deep alcove in a limestone cliff.

In the 1970s, solar energy enthusiasts made pilgrimages to study the castle: Its graceful concave facade is perfectly designed to fetch the most winter sunlight possible and fend off the midday summer sun. Whoever they were, the Sinagua knew something about architecture.

Tuzigoot, too, is a marvelous piece of work, anticipating by 800 years Frank Lloyd Wright's dictum that "No house should ever be on any hill . . . it should be of the hill." The village follows the contours of a 100-foot-high ridge overlooking the Verde River with such consummate grace that the hill would seem unfinished today without it. It seems unlikely, however, that the Tuzigootians had aesthetics in mind. It would have been safe from the Verde's periodic flooding, and the high ground provided wary people a natural lookout.

An interesting footnote is that the people of Tuzigoot apparently became more wary over time. At some point, ground-floor doorways were sealed, leaving only rooftop entrances. By the time the pueblo was abandoned around 1425, there was just one outside doorway for 77 ground-floor rooms.

This and a few other tantalizing clues caused me to spend a good part of six years panning for evidence of the prehistoric war that either dispersed or killed off not only the Sinagua, but also every other major culture in Arizona between 1250 and 1450. But there was no great war. There just came to be too many people for a fragile environment to support — a disarmingly simple explanation that reverberates around the increasingly crowded red rocks today.

Jerome

"The Wickedest Town in America," hissed the *New York Sun* in 1903. Not about its hometown, but about tiny Jerome, Arizona, a rickety mountainside village 2,000 miles west of New York and a hundred miles north of Phoenix. Not only was the place rife with boozing, wenching, brawling, and gambling, reported the newspaper; it also was ugly, noisy, congested, and polluted. "The best thing that could happen to Jerome," the *Sun* snarled, "would be a nice, big, citywide fire."

The *Sun's* tirade was reprinted locally and was greeted with predictable howls of outrage. Read it today, and it seems funny and ironic — New York, the pot, scolding this harmless kettle of a town for its pollution and immorality. But the writer was not far wrong. Jerome, in its mining years, was truly a hell of a place to live and work.

"We have a tendency to romanticize mining and mining towns here in the West," said

Arizona historian James W. Byrkit, who grew up three miles downslope in Clarkdale. "But there was never anything romantic about Jerome."

Nevertheless, the romanticism is in full bloom today. Jerome has become a major attraction, an essential stop for tour buses on the Prescott-Sedona-Grand Canyon swing. And there are good reasons to come here, though not all the locals appreciate the throngs in the streets.

Jerome was born with a copper mining claim in 1876. A rudimentary mining camp quickly sprang up around the first shafts. In 1883, the United Verde Copper Company built the camp's first smelter. Ten years later, a narrow-gauge railway replaced the 20-mule freight wagons that had been groaning over 7,743-foot Mingus Mountain. Jerome then was ready for civilization of a sort.

But not since the Anasazi cliff dwellings of 1250 had an American settlement been so improbably located. Jerome's Victorian houses and hotels were stitched onto the side of Mingus Mountain, every building site a 10- or 20-percent grade. Main Street's switchbacks resembled a snake doubled up with stomach gas. In 1899, a Phoenix newspaperman noted that "your neighbor to the rear, in Jerome, can't look into your back windows, although he can look down your kitchen chimney from his front porch."

Still, by 1900, Jerome claimed 2,681 residents, which made it the fifth largest town in Arizona Territory. It was no longer a mining camp, but a place with at least the veneer of civilization. The Montana Hotel, which opened that year, was a handsome, carefully detailed, four-story Georgian Revival building that would have been quite at home in Boston. It's architecture helped convince inhabitants and visitors that Jerome was for real. By this time, the mines were throwing off enough copper, silver, and gold that the town was attracting some serious cigars.

But the high style was an illusion. Jerome wasn't stable or sophisticated. It was raw, tough, precarious, dangerous, and yes, wicked.

Spindly wooden buildings stacked practically atop one another made Jerome a firetrap. Devastating blazes swept through town in 1894, '97, '98, '99, 1902, '07, '11, and '15 — the last fire claiming the grand Montana. There also were floods, mudslides, epidemics of smallpox and scarlet fever, street violence, and, most of all, the mine work itself. Hear Byrkit again. It was never romantic. Between 1895 and 1935, despite the claims of United Verde executives that "everything possible was being done [for safety]," about 150 miners lost their lives in the man-made bowels of Mingus Mountain. This was the true wickedness of Jerome.

The ore vein was essentially vertical, and the main shaft plunged 4,650 feet into the mountain. At the bottom was the foyer of hell.

Byrkit, son of a mine executive, recalled a boyhood visit in the 1940s: "The miners were in rubber boots, working in water about a foot deep. It was humid and very, very hot — I would guess over 100°. They could work only 20 minutes without a rest."

Prostitution was a major industry in Jerome, maybe second only to mining. It was intermittently legal and

Fires and mudslides destroyed
most of Jerome's original
buildings, but the entire town
is a historic landmark.
George H.H. Huey

regulated, with the "girls"
required to report for biweekly
medical exams. There were
opium dens, gambling houses,
and scores of saloons,
occasionally featuring bands or
vaudeville acts. There was a
chronic shortage of rooms for
the miners, so they rented
rooms and bunks in shifts. A
miners' circadian rhythm
evolved: eight hours working,
eight hours drinking, eight hours
sleeping, the clock segments
interchangeable depending on
which shift one spent
underground.

Jerome was a goulash of
ethnicity, far more interesting
than the big towns of Phoenix
and Tucson at the time. In 1918,
the United Verde issued a
nationality report on its Jerome
employees, revealing that those
born on U.S. soil were a
minority. There were 401
Mexicans, 393 Americans, 96
Slavs, 68 Spaniards, 60
Austrians, 57 Italians, 53 Irish,
and 32 Serbs. Ethnic tensions
were not unknown, but down in
the mine, at least, the men
worked as brothers. Their lives
depended on it.

For a boomtown, Jerome
had an unusually long life. With
the end of World War I and the
decline in demand for copper
jackets for bullets, the mining
went on, but at a slowing pace.
Finally, in 1953, the mine shut

down. In 77 years, Mingus
Mountain had given up an
estimated $1 billion in copper,
gold, silver, zinc, and lead.

In a universe driven by logic
and not sentiment, Jerome
would have died right then.
There never had been any
industry but mining, and there
was no reason for anyone to
stay. The population evaporated
to around 100, and only a few
businesses hung on — a couple
of bars, a rock shop, an antique
store. But then a handful of
people formed the Jerome
Historical Society, believing that
the story of this colorful, wicked
town was worth preserving.

Jerome's revival began
tentatively around 1970. A few
people who lived in the town
during the mining years
returned to retire. Then a few

bohemians and artists discovered it. The preposterously low cost of living and rim-of-the-world views off Mingus Mountain were major attractions.

Nancy Smith, an unofficial town historian and former city council member, recalled coming to Jerome in 1972: "The younger people lived in apartment buildings (formerly miners' boarding houses), with an agreement that we would take care of minor things and not bother the owners with a lot of complaints. These people didn't need a lot of money to live, and they provided an inexpensive labor force for restoration. My situation was typical: I moved into an attic apartment with one of the most fantastic views in the world — and it was $25 a month."

Jerome today is Arizona's oddest town. The population is still tiny — between 410 and 490, depending on whom you ask. Most of the 1890-1915 buildings are gone, victims of the fires or mudslides. But there are still about 300 historic houses and commercial buildings standing (the whole town resides on the National Register of Historic Places). Many have been lovingly restored; a few still stand as silent ruins. And Jerome still draws dreamers, bohemians, and artists looking for inspiration and cheap work space. One gallery owner estimated that 100 of Jerome's 400-something residents are artists, musicians, or writers.

Robin John Anderson is one of the more prominent artists. For their studio and gallery, he and his wife, Margo Mandette,

lease an 18,000-square-foot school built in 1911. Even today, their rent is just $3,000 a month.

"I started feeling kind of isolated a few years ago, so I went to New York," Anderson says. "But the filth, the congestion, the social problems — I had to come back to this island of serenity."

Yet the town remains endearingly schizophrenic: raffish and stylish, tawdry and cutesy, and seldom hesitant to laugh at itself. One gallery peddles $1 earrings, another devotes itself entirely to cat crafts, and then there's Tracy Weisel's thoroughly sophisticated Raku Gallery, which could have been transplanted straight from San Francisco. In general, art buyers can still find more eclecticism and eccentricity — and lower

prices — than they can in Sedona. The overhead is lower; the risk-taking is higher.

Another turn of eccentricity is the House of Joy, which connoisseurs have considered one of Arizona's best restaurants ever since it opened in a retired bordello in 1969. It's open only Saturday and Sunday evenings, and it can take several months to finagle a reservation. No restaurant in Arizona has a more wicked sign out front: a shapely, promising, red-gartered leg kicking out of a second-story window. Still another: the Holy Family Catholic Church, whose painted wooden neo-Gothic reredos has a folk-art charm about it. The story behind the

Choices for shoppers in Jerome are eclectic and eccentric.
Tom Bean

church's restoration is a Jerome classic. When the Rev. Juan Atucha, the last full-time pastor, died in 1979, parishioners found about $60,000 in change and small bills stashed about the rectory and church. He'd been hoarding it, apparently, for 30 years. Thanks to his eccentricity, the church was restored the following year.

Not everybody in Jerome welcomes the town's renewed notoriety. But Nancy Smith says she watches the tourists with little anguish; she believes that Jerome will always be Jerome.

"The historic character will be preserved, no matter what," she says. "We have the laws in place now to keep it that way. The other thing is my old belief that the town will survive, no matter who comes here. Jerome just has a way of casting off people who aren't quite right for it."

The Verde Valley

Downslope from Jerome, the Verde River glides through sandstone canyons and forests of sycamore and cottonwood trees en route to an eventual rendezvous with the Salt River east of Phoenix. The towns strung through the valley — Clarkdale, Cottonwood, Cornville, Camp Verde — are beginning to nourish arts communities of their own as Sedona becomes more expensive.

Recreation and history are offered in three state parks. Dead Horse Ranch's 320

The Verde River nourishes towns such as Clarkdale and stands of cottonwoods and sycamores alike. Bob & Suzanne Clemenz

Top: This lagoon is a central feature
at Dead Horse Ranch State Park.
George Stocking
Above: The Verde Canyon Railroad
ventures into a canyon loaded with
scenery and wildlife. Tom Johnson
Left: Fort Verde State Historic Park
traces its origins to a fort built in 1871.
Richard Maack

riparian acres provide an engaging venue for birding, picnicking, or canoeing along the Verde River. Jerome State Historic Park, housed in an 8,000-square-foot mansion built in 1916 by mine magnate James S. Douglas, displays Mingus Mountain's mining history. Fort Verde State Historic Park is a U.S. Army fort built in 1871 to subdue the Yavapai and Apache, who were troubling the Anglos newly arrived to farm and ranch the valley. One visitor's comment in the guest register seemed to say it all: "A good exhibit on a sad part of American history."

One of the valley's most popular captivations is the Verde Canyon Railroad, which carries about 60,000 passengers a year on a 12-mile-an-hour dawdle from Clarkdale to the nearly nonexistent settlement of Perkinsville and back. One of its chief attractions is nostalgia: On every excursion there's a grandparent who used to ride the train and a grandchild who's never before been aboard one. The other is scenery. The train rumbles through woodlands, where the cottonwood canopies

span 50 feet, and then into a deepening canyon where the rufous sandstone walls eventually tower 700 feet above the train. Great blue herons and golden and bald eagles winter in the canyon, joining year-round resident javelinas, beavers, river otters, mountain lions, bobcats, black bears, and wild turkeys. There's no other way to see this; the railroad is the only road into the canyon.

A prehistoric civilization, a

A snowy Mingus Mountain presides over Cottonwood, basking in the the ample sunshine of the Verde Valley.
Bob & Suzanne Clemenz

painful chapter in the building of America, a wicked Victorian mining town, a slow train into a vanished past — the Verde Valley seems so young, and yet a thousand years of human history lies right on its surface, taking in the abundant sun.

When You Go

Jerome And The Verde Valley   Most of the valley lies at an elevation of 3,300 to 3,500 feet —1,000 feet lower than Sedona — so expect a hot summer and a mild winter.

For tourist information: Cottonwood-Verde Valley Chamber of Commerce, (520) 634-7593. Jerome Chamber of Commerce, (520) 634-2900. Camp Verde Chamber of Commerce, (520) 567-9294. Jerome has a Web site at http://www.sedona.net/jerome/

Dead Horse Ranch State Park, (520) 634-5283. Fort Verde State Historic Park, (520) 567-3275. Jerome State Historic Park, (520) 634-5381.

The Verde Canyon Railroad offers excursions leaving Clarkdale at 11 A.M. daily except some Mondays and Tuesdays, depending on season. Saturday night starlight rides run from June through October. Reservations required for all excursions. (800) 293-7245 or (520) 639-0010.

CHAPTER FIVE

Farther Out

*Excursions to the Grand Canyon,
Mogollon Rim, and Navajoland*

Destination, Grand
Canyon. The itinerary
of many Sedona
visitors takes them
there, to the Rim or
down into it.
Top: Rafters plunge
through Hermit Rapid
on the Colorado River.
Kerrick James

Above: From Yaki Point
on the South Rim,
sunset fires the
emotions of watchers.
Tom Bean
Opposite page:
Sunrise bathes Cape
Royal on the North Rim.
George Stocking

*With the rainbow hanging high
on the ends of your wings, come
to us soaring.*
— NAVAJO NIGHT CHANT
(1902 English translation)

These excursions are overnighters, because they encompass too many miles and too many sensations to fold into a single day. The Grand Canyon is only 120 miles away, but most of those miles are congested, so figure three hours each way.

Grand Canyon
Former Arizona Governor Bruce Babbitt told this revealing story in a Grand Canyon anthology he edited 20 years ago: He was standing near a clump of tourists at the South Rim as a world-class sunset ripened over the Canyon. One of them snapped a Polaroid, and the rest all turned away from the sky to watch the image of it develop.

The Canyon and its skies are so overwhelming, so far outside the range of other human experience, that our senses at first refuse to comprehend.

Which is the prime argument for spending serious time with the Canyon — hiking it, rafting it, photographing it, sitting on the Rim in quiet meditation at sunrise or sunset.

One needs "To step off the brink," as Babbitt wrote, "and to get personally involved in the demanding reality of the Canyon."

A two-day excursion to the South Rim from Sedona could conveniently take in the Museum of Northern Arizona en route, a full afternoon and evening on the South Rim, and an all-day hike into the Canyon the following day on Bright Angel or South Kaibab trail. Very strong hikers can make the trip to the Canyon floor and back in a day (elevation gain 4,600 feet), but the return to Sedona would call for a designated driver.

Mogollon Rim

There are countless places in Arizona where one can go to contemplate the Apache wars, but none is more dramatically scenic than a little-known gravel logging road that closely follows the trail that Gen. George Crook blazed along the edge of the Mogollon Rim some 130 years ago.

It was here on an August afternoon in 1872 that Crook and his men were scouting the terrain and blazing a supply trail when the Tonto Apaches introduced themselves with a blizzard of arrows. The soldiers scrambled for cover and returned fire, and most of the Apaches melted back into the forest. Two of them, trapped right on the lip of the 2,000-foot escarpment by the soldiers, fired

The Apache wars burned the Mogollon Rim into Arizona's history. Dick Dietrich

85

their last arrows in defiance, then leaped over the rim, apparently choosing suicide over capture. When Crook's men rushed over, they saw two Apaches leaping "like mountain sheep" from rock to rock. Because of encounters like this, Crook developed a profound respect for the people he was under orders to subdue.

It's a 215-mile round trip from Sedona to the scenic drive along Forest Service Road 300, which parallels the rim. The gravel road is fine for passenger cars in dry weather but is usually closed to all traffic in winter. From Sedona, take State Route 179 and Interstate 17 to Camp Verde and drive east on State Route 260 to State Route 87. Turn left (north) and drive a few miles for the turnoff for FR 300 — on the right, just beyond

Milepost 281. The forest road intersects State Route 260 a little more than 30 miles east of Payson. Montezuma Castle, Fort Verde State Historic Park, and Tonto Natural Bridge State Park all lie conveniently along the loop.

Navajoland

The Navajo Reservation, or Navajo Nation, is almost twice the size of Switzerland and at least as resplendent in natural and cultural attractions. A three-day loop from Sedona would cover about 550 miles, taking in the possibilities of Navajo National Monument, Monument Valley, Canyon de Chelly, Hubbell Trading Post, and as a bonus, nearby Petrified Forest National Park. Another premium on this excursion is

Above: Betatakin, a 135-room dwelling built by the Anasazi, seems to flow out of the cliff at Navajo National Monument.
Tom Danielsen
Opposite page: As the sun rises, the shadows of stone monoliths dance across Monument Valley. This view looks north from Hunts Mesa.
Robert G. McDonald

inevitable contact with the Diné, the People, as the Navajos call themselves. I have always found Navajos to be wonderfully direct and engaging. If you approach with genuine interest and respect, Navajos will talk with you openly.

Navajo National Monument includes the most extravagant and best-preserved Anasazi ruins in Arizona, but they are open only in summer and require both advance planning and sweat to

Right: White House Ruin
remains a timeless memorial
to prehistoric people who
lived in Canyon de Chelly.
Dick Dietrich
Below: The old ways are still
a way of life in Monument Valley:
A lone Navajo woman tends sheep
and a rider and members of his
family drive a flock across the sand.
Both by Edward McCain

see. Betatakin is a five-mile round-trip hike; Keet Seel is 17 miles round trip by foot. Both are well worth the effort.

Canyon de Chelly National Monument secretes about 400 Anasazi ruins in an awesomely beautiful canyon system shaped like a giant bird's gnarled footprint. Only one ruin, the White House, is accessible without a guide. Very highly recommended: Half- or all-day vehicle or horseback tours of the canyon floor with Navajo guides. Paved roads overlooking the south rim (36 miles round trip) and north rim (34 miles) are also well worth the time.

Monument Valley is a Navajo tribal park, not U.S. government property, and it, too, is experienced most intimately with a native guide. Visitors on their own may drive the park's 17-mile loop, but do not venture off-road to hike, picnic, or camp without a guide.

Hubbell Trading Post at Ganado was founded in 1876 and is still open for business as a privately owned National Historic Site. Bargains in Navajo rugs are now memories as

Right: Hubbell Trading Post has been serving the Navajo people as supplier, banker, and buyer of their goods for more than 120 years.
Jerry Jacka
Opposite page: Petrified logs form a unique landscape in Jasper Forest in the Petrified Forest National Park.
Larry Ulrich

ancient as nickel Cokes, but the quantity and quality of Hubbell's selection is staggering, and worth a special stop, if only for dreaming.

Petrified Forest National Park is famous, of course, for its unique landscape litter of 225-million-year-old logs. The park's prehistoric Anasazi ruins are modest, but an unadvertised special is one of the most concentrated petroglyph collections in Arizona. Walk south across the mesa from the

Puerco Ruin and look among the rocks at the foot of the slope.

"OBVIOUS ARIZONA," Vladimir Nabokov called it in *Lolita*, this land of polychrome earth, yawning blue canyons, and sculpted red rocks. The images are obvious because they're so familiar; in the world's eyes, they are Arizona. But the land continues to make promises to the human spirit and to reward a lifetime's acquaintance. The closing lines of the Navajo Night Chant capture the essence of this relationship:

With beauty before me,
I walk.
With beauty behind me,
I walk.
With beauty below me,
I walk.
With beauty above me,
I walk.
With beauty all around me,
I walk.
It is finished in beauty.

When You Go

For general Grand Canyon National Park information, call (520) 638-7888. For accommodations inside the park, call (520) 638-2401. There are also motels at Tusayan, 10 miles from the South Rim visitors center.

For information regarding the suggested Mogollon Rim excursion: Montezuma Castle National Monument, (520) 567-3322. Fort Verde State Historic Park, (520) 567-3275. Tonto Natural Bridge State Park, (520) 476-4202. Payson Chamber of Commerce, (520) 474-4515 or (800) 6-PAYSON (672-9766).

For general inquiries about traveling on the Navajo Reservation, call the Navajo Tourism Department at Tribal Headquarters in Window Rock, (520) 871-6659. Navajo National Monument, (520) 672-2367. Monument Valley, (801) 727-3287. Canyon de Chelly National Monument, (520) 674-5500. Hubbell Trading Post National Historic Site, (520) 755-3254. Petrified Forest National Park, (520) 524-6228.

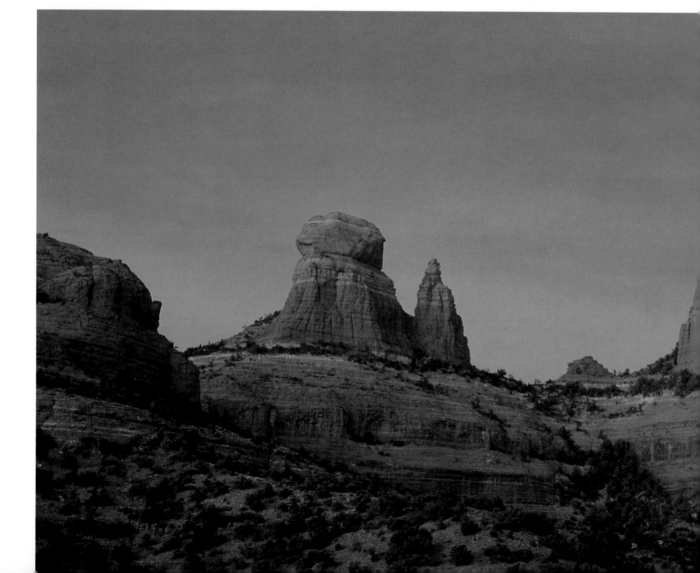

These formations and ridgeline identify Bear Wallow Canyon, which runs along a portion of Schnebly Hill Road.
Steve Bruno
Following pages 94 and 95:
This view is from the trail leading up Wilson Mountain just north of Sedona. Ship Rock is at left. Larry Lindahl

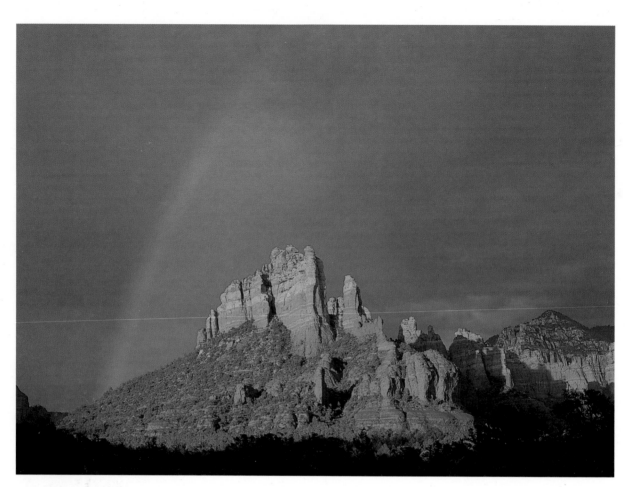

Camel Head Rock literally
glows in the setting sun
after a storm. Tom Bean

Cover: The allure of Sedona
and red rock country embraces
Cathedral Rock, in the foreground,
and Oak Creek Canyon, with the
San Francisco Peaks on the horizon.
Adriel Heisey
Inside Front Cover: The stately
Courthouse Butte tops a knoll
with a thicket of mesquite trees
and yucca plants.
Randy Prentice
Inside Back Cover: One of
Sedona's classic scenes: Red Rock
Crossing on Oak Creek with
Cathedral Rock overlooking it.
Kerrick James
Back Cover: A hiker heads for
solitude along the West Fork Creek
in the Red Rock-Secret Mountain
Wilderness. Tom Bean